THE
RIVIERA
REFERENCE BOOK

DEALER
BULLETINS FOR

 # BUICK

———1963-1974———

RIVIERA

THE
RIVIERA
REFERENCE BOOK

American Musclecar Publications

—CONTENTS—

BUICK RIVIERA 1964-1973
—TECHNICAL SERVICE BULLETINS—

—ACKNOWLEDGEMENTS—

We Gratefully Acknowledge the following people and organizations for their contributions to this book:

Buick Motor Division; Buick Public Relations for Photographs; John Draghich for his help on finding these Bulletins; Poston Enterprises for Distribution and faith in us; D. Armstrong Book Printing for their help on Book Publishing.

The Riviera Club of America; The Gran Sport Club of America and The Buick Club of America; Walter Kruger for layout and other input; Don Pharass for help on the printing process. This Book simply could not have been written without the help of those mentioned.

We sincerely thank all of you and any others we may have overlooked.

Sincerely
Steven Dove
Author

—INTRODUCTION—

Material such as that in this Reference Book has become very difficult to find, especially in complete sets of all Technical Bulletins and Product Reports on Buicks. However, after researching for many years, we were able to complete a set of Buick Bulletins for the years 1964-1973.

These Bulletins have some of the most interesting and useful information we have ever read on the Riviera and Big Buick. After reading through these bulletins, we figured that other Riviera and Big Buick enthusiasts would most likely find the same interest that we did. The information that they contain, simply cannot be found from any other source.

There are many Riviera and Big Buick Enthusiasts and Collectors that really appreciate these great cars. Most of us love to find rare, original information about our cars. To document most of these Rare Dealer Technical Bulletins and Product Reports on Rivieras into one Volume was an exciting adventure. Indeed, to have a year by year reference source of this kind was our goal.

Even though it was impossible to include every single bulletin we had into this volume, we read through each year and chose what we thought would be the most useful, interesting and informative. With over 200 pages, we have compiled a very comprehensive Reference Source for all Buick Rivieras from 1964-1973 with some 1963 bulletins included in the 1964 chapter.

INTRODUCTION

The Bulletins themselves were used by Buick to inform their Dealers of all technical problems and changes that may have occurred in each model year. They also introduced new or different products to their dealers. They often went into great detail with many pages of illustrations and pictures. Sometimes, over 25 pages may have been used; one example was the introduction of the 1965 Gran Sport, which consisted of over 30 pages!

This book commences with the year 1964 and goes through 1973. Each year makes up a new Chapter with a total of 9 chapters in all. Additionally, there are many pictures of Rivieras throughout the book.

Since the purpose of this book is to document as many Technical Bulletins as possible on the Buick Riviera, no other information is included; however, we are currently writing the Riviera Facts & Figures Book that will cover many other subjects on the Riviera. These two books are written to compliment each other. Further, we will update this book in later editions with any new bulletins that become available to us.

We sincerely wish that you the Enthusiast, will see the value of having these Rare Technical Bulletins in one handy source. Moreover, we hope that this book will be interesting and useful to you for a long time.

Thank you
Steven L. Dove
Author 6-2-91

CHAPTER ONE

1964 RIVIERA

BUICK DEALER
SERVICE
INFORMATION

Dealer Letter No.   File Under Group No.

65-19   1-2

BUICK MOTOR DIVISION   GENERAL MOTORS CORPORATION   FLINT, MICHIGAN 48550

October 2, 1964

TO ALL BUICK DEALERS

SUBJECT: Factory Engine Oil Recommendations

In recent months, failed parts being returned to the factory indicate, in some cases, that engine oils meeting the Service MS requirements and passing car makers' tests (such as GM 4745M) are <u>not</u> being used by customers. Today's modern Buick engines create higher operating temperatures because of high speed and stop-go driving, increased number of engine-powered accessories (such as air conditioning), and higher compression ratios.

In addition, when short-trip operation occurs regularly during the winter months, engine oil does not always have a chance to completely warm up. When this happens, rapid oil dilution is encountered with consequent corrosion of internal parts. Detrimental effects of this nature can only be minimized by using oils which are marked, "For Service MS" and "Passes Car Makers' Tests".

The following definitions of engine oil types, as set forth by the petroleum industry, will further clarify the reasons for recommending only Service MS oils.

Designation	Definition
ML	Service typical of gasoline and other spark ignition engines operating <u>under light and favorable service conditions</u>, the engines having no special lubrication requirements and having no design characteristics sensitive to deposit formation.
MM	Service typical of gasoline and other spark ignition engines operating <u>under moderate to severe service conditions</u>, but presenting problems of deposit or bearing corrosion control when crankcase oil temperatures are high.
MS	Service typical of gasoline or other spark ignition engines operating <u>under unfavorable or severe types of service conditions</u>, and where there are special lubrication requirements for deposit or bearing corrosion control, due to operating conditions or to fuel or to engine design characteristics.

It should be stressed to customers that the recommendations in the Owner Guides regarding oil selection are the results of years of testing and experience, and should be kept in mind when selecting a motor oil. Incorrect oil selection can result in premature piston ring and bearing wear, oil sludging, and excessive oil consumption.

E. J. Hresko
Manager, Technical Service

2

Dealer Letter No.	File Under Group No.
64-176	2-19

BUICK
DEALER SERVICE
INFORMATION

BUICK MOTOR DIVISION, GENERAL MOTORS CORPORATION, FLINT 2, MICHIGAN

August 14, 1964

TO ALL BUICK DEALERS

SUBJECT: Oil Economy - 425 Cubic Inch Engine

We have received dealer requests for a statement from the factory as to what is considered to be normal oil economy on a 425 cubic inch engine. This statement can best be answered if specific driving conditions to which the car is subjected are known. It's like asking, what is the normal fuel economy for any given model. If there were not so many variables involved, a simple specific statement could be offered. We tried to answer this oil economy question by including the article below in our recent Dealer Service Letter 64-158, dated June 5, 1964.

Our Engineering Department is in agreement with the information presented in this article, and since it is a down-to-earth reply, we are again, for your information, quoting it below.

"A gasoline engine depends upon oil to lubricate the cylinder walls, pistons, and piston rings. When the piston moves downward, a thin film of oil is left on the cylinder walls, and on the firing stroke it is burned by the flame of combustion. If an engine burned as much as one drop of oil on every firing stroke, then it would use more than a quart every two miles. Such consumption is unheard of in the automotive field, but all efficient engines use some oil. If they did not, they would quickly wear out.

"The rate of consumption depends upon the quality and viscosity of the oil, the speed at which the engine is operated, the temperature and the amount of dilution and oxidation which takes place. These conditions are frequently misleading. An example of this is where a car has run 1000 miles or more in city operation, has consumed a normal amount of oil, but actually measures up to the full mark due to dilution in the crankcase. The car then might be driven at high speed on the highway, the dilution elements boil off rapidly, and the car appears to use two quarts of oil in a hundred miles.

"Car owners should expect greatly increased oil consumption at high speeds. For instance, it is a proven fact that an automotive engine may use seven times the quantity of oil at 70 than it does at 40 miles per hour. No standard rate of consumption can be established because under various combinations of the conditions mentioned above, one engine might use a quart in 1500 miles and another use a quart in 750 miles and yet both engines might be entirely normal.

"New engines require considerable running before the piston rings and cylinder walls become 'conditioned', and during this time they use oil more rapidly than later. An engine's oil economy should not be judged until it has run at least 4000 miles."

Keeping the above article in mind, we would like to present the following information before making a general statement on 425 cu. in. engine oil economy.

1. Our engineers, as well as those of other manufacturers, are constantly trying to improve designs which will effectively provide improved oil economy, as well as maintain or increase reliability of the engine.

2. Engines having large bore diameters subject the piston rings to greater sealing area which becomes more critical to control oil economy. This applies to any engine. As the bore diameter increases above 4 inches, it becomes more difficult for the rings to perform their function.

3. The more powerful the engine, the more important lubrication becomes. The engine is providing more power, and if adequate lubrication was not available, parts would become worn and the reliability and life of the engine greatly reduced.

4. Some manufacturers recommend single viscosity SAE 20 and even SAE 30 weight oils during Summer operation which helps overcome the oil economy loss on these super-powered engines. This recommendation also can be applied to our engines as long as the oil has the designation "MS" on its container. At temperatures below plus 32°F. lighter oils should be used as recommended in the owners manual.

Our powerful 425 cubic inch engines, which produce a maximum 465 pound feet of torque at 2800 RPM, one of the highest in the industry for low and mid-range torque, will, under normal driving conditions, average 700 to 800 miles per quart. This rate on the 425 cubic inch engine compares favorably with other high performance engines on the market today.

Owner complaints of two to three quarts per 1000 miles when encountered should be carefully investigated and the economy verified before attempting corrective measures. Experience has shown that in many instances when verification is made, the oil economy is within the range of 700 to 800 miles per quart.

Also, in some instances, the owner wants assurance that the oil economy will not become worse. Oil economy will not become worse, so please explain this and give them this assurance. All of us agree if the facts are known, then there is little concern and owner's mind is at ease.

W. M. McCrocklin
General Service Manager

BUICK DEALER
SERVICE
INFORMATION

Dealer Letter No.   File Under Group No.

65-28   10-4

BUICK MOTOR DIVISION   GENERAL MOTORS CORPORATION   FLINT, MICHIGAN 48550

October 9, 1964

TO ALL BUICK DEALERS

SUBJECT: Riviera Head Lamp Visors

During the public showing of our 1965 Buicks, the comment was heard from
several prospects, "I wonder how the Riviera headlamps will operate after
being subjected to ice, snow, mud, etc." We believe this is a normal re-
action to something as new as the 1965 Riviera headlamp visors and that we
can continue to expect to hear similar comments throughout the 1965 model
year.

We want to assure you that the Riviera visors have been thoroughly tested
and are designed to operate satisfactorily, even under the most adverse
conditions. So that all dealer personnel may be prepared to reply to the
type comment quoted above, we offer you the following information:

1. During the development of the 1965 Riviera, the headlamp visors were
    subjected to freezing rain, ice, slush and snow, and in no case did we
    experience a failure due to these conditions. The Rivieras were driven
    in slushy snow to pack as much around the visors as possible. These
    cars were then parked and temperatures dropped to zero degrees. This
    was done to create the worst possible condition and try to freeze the
    visors. Even under these conditions, the visors operated without any
    difficulty.

2. To provide a more severe test, a spray of water was manually directed
    on the visors to build up as much ice as possible when outside tempera-
    ture was below zero. Ice was packed approximately 1/8" thick all over
    the visor by squirting a flow of water horizontally on the visors during
    the zero degree temperature.

    It was only under these man-made conditions that we were able to stick
    the visors. However, only one light tap of the hand on each visor was
    necessary to break the ice loose.

    We would like to point out that these same Rivieras were subjected to
    natural freezing rain and the visors operated without any difficulty
    whatsoever.

3. The Riviera headlamps are protected by the fender and have been purposely
    recessed inward far enough to eliminate malfunction due to ice and snow.

5

4. The Rivieras were driven through numerous mud baths at the General Motors Proving Grounds and the visors still operated satisfactorily.

5. Some other manufacturers have had malfunctions due to ice, but their design was such that the visors were not protected from above.

It is only through a knowledgeable Dealer Sales and Service Organization that we can expect an outstanding selling job and we hope the above information will assist you in selling more Rivieras in 1965.

W. M. McCrocklin
General Service Manager

6

BUICK
DEALER SERVICE
INFORMATION

Dealer Letter No.	File Under Group No.
65-15	10-1

BUICK MOTOR DIVISION, GENERAL MOTORS CORPORATION, FLINT 2, MICHIGAN

September 25, 1964

TO ALL BUICK DEALERS

SUBJECT: Riviera Headlamp Visors

The following headlamp visor check (4 steps) must be added to the New Car Pre-Delivery Inspection on all 1965 Rivieras. This check is important because improperly adjusted visors may not allow the visor motor to shut off, causing a continuous drain on the battery.

CHECKING PROCEDURE

1. With headlamps off, make sure visor doors on both sides are fully closed. If one or both visors are not closed fully, adjust visor linkage as described in step A.

2. Obtain a test light having a sharp prod. With one test lead grounded, pierce the brown wire and the black wire leading to the visor motor. See figure 1.

FIGURE 1

7

If test lamp lights from only one wire, visor closing cycle is okay; if test lamp lights from both wires, correct trouble as described in step B.

3. Turn on headlamps. Make sure visor doors open. If visor does not open, correct trouble as described in step C.

4. Again pierce both brown wire and black wire with test prod. See figure 1. If test lamp lights from only one wire, visor opening cycle is okay; if test lamp lights from both wires, correct trouble as described in step D.

ADJUSTING PROCEDURES

STEP A. <u>One or Both Visors Not Closed</u>

If one or both visors do not close fully, it may be necessary to adjust the linkage to both visors. This initial linkage adjustment is made with the motor arm positioned about 5° before the end of its normal closing cycle; the additional 5° closing movement of the arm provides a "crush" at the visors to insure full closing. Adjust linkage as follows:

1. Open visors by turning on headlamps.

2. Hold a .020" feeler gauge between the motor arm and the rear limit switch; then close visors. See figure 2.

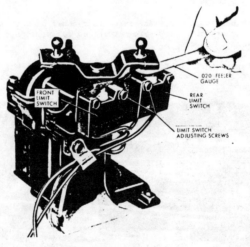

FIGURE 2

3. Loosen both adjusting bolts on horizontal links. See figure 3. Check for a bind in either linkage; <u>eliminate any bind before proceeding</u>.

4. Close visor on one side by hand and tighten adjusting bolt on that side; perform same operation on other side.

5. Open visors and remove .020" feeler gauge. Close visors and check visors for full closing.

-2-

8

STEP B. <u>Motor Not Off with Visors Closed</u>

If test light shows voltage is present in both the brown wire and the
black wire with the visors closed, this means that the rear limit switch
on the motor is not depressed by the arm to shut off the motor; instead,
the motor is stopped by the visor linkage, but the current is not shut off
because the limit switch is not reached. See figure 4 for theory of operation. Correction is made as follows:

1. Open visors slightly by hand to see which side feels tightest. Loosen
    adjusting bolt on horizontal link on that side just enough so that
    bolt slips slightly in adjusting slot. Retighten bolt. See figure 3.

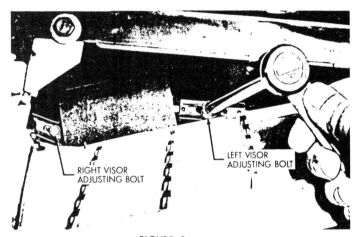

FIGURE 3

2. Open visors by turning on headlamps.

    CAUTION: <u>It may be necessary to wait up to 45 seconds for circuit</u>
              <u>breaker in motor to close before motor will operate. (See</u>
              <u>last paragraph of bulletin for explanation.)</u>

3. Close visors by turning off headlamps.

4. Use test light to check for voltage in both the brown wire and the
    black wire. If voltage is now present in only one wire, the linkage
    is now adjusted correctly, allowing the motor arm to rotate farther
    and depress the rear limit switch.

5. If the test light check shows that voltage is still present in both
    wires, repeat the above procedure on the tightest side until the rear
    limit switch is depressed when the visors are closed.

6. If any amount of linkage adjustment will still not cause the motor arm
    to depress the rear limit switch, the arm may be bent upward. If a
    bent arm is found, straighten arm and start checking procedure from
    the beginning.

-3-

9

7. If motor arm is not bent, then the rear limit switch must be adjusted too low. Loosen the forward (adjusting) screw slightly, move the switch up slightly and retighten the screw. See figure 2.

   CAUTION: Do not tighten screw too tight or it will crack switch body.

   NOTE: Switches should be adjusted only as a last resort as this adjustment is very difficult.

STEP C. One or Both Visors Not Open

If one or both visors do not open, it may be necessary to adjust the linkage to both visors. The linkage must always be adjusted at the end of the closed cycle as described in step A.

During the adjustment, while the adjusting bolts are loose, make sure the linkage to both visors is free of binds. Make sure visors do not strike inside the fender while opening or closing.

STEP D. Motor Not Off with Visors Open

If test light shows voltage is present in both the brown wire and the black wire with the visors open, this means that the forward limit switch on the motor is not depressed by the arm to shut off the motor; instead, the motor is stopped by the visor linkage, but the current is not shut off because the limit switch is not reached. See figure 5 for theory of operation. Correction is made as follows:

1. Close visors slightly by hand to see which side feels tightest. Loosen adjusting bolt on that side just enough so that bolt slips slightly in adjusting slot. Retighten bolt. See figure 3.

2. Close visors by turning off headlamps.

   CAUTION: It may be necessary to wait up to 45 seconds for circuit breaker in motor to close before motor will operate. (See last paragraph for explanation.)

3. Open visors by turning on headlamps.

4. Use test light to check for voltage in both the brown wire and the black wire. If voltage is now present in only one wire, the linkage is now adjusted correctly, allowing the motor arm to rotate farther and depress the forward limit switch.

5. If the test light check shows that voltage is still present in both wires, repeat the above procedure on the tightest side until the forward switch is depressed when the visors are open.

6. If any amount of linkage adjustment will still not cause the motor arm to depress the front limit switch, the arm may be bent upward. If a bent arm is found, straighten arm and start checking procedure from the beginning.

7. If motor arm is not bent, then the front limit switch may be adjusted too low. Loosen the rear (adjusting) screw slightly, move the switch up slightly and retighten the screw. See figure 2.

   CAUTION: Do not tighten screw too tight or it will crack switch body.

   NOTE: Switches should be adjusted only as a last resort, as this adjustment is very difficult.

-4-

VISOR ELECTRICAL CIRCUITS

During the headlamp visor closing cycle, current is supplied from the junction block, through a circuit breaker and a red wire to a visor control relay. See figure 4. The relay armature spring holds the armature in the up position, where it connects to a black wire. The black wire leads to the visor motor where the current enters through the rear limit switch mounted on the upper end of the motor. The current flows through the closing field and armature, causing the armature to rotate in a direction to close the visors. When the visors are closed tight, the motor arm depresses the rear limit switch, thereby opening the circuit.

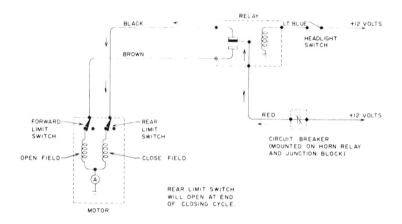

CLOSING CYCLE

FIGURE 4

During the visor opening cycle, the headlamps must be switched on. Current is supplied through the same red wire to the relay. See figure 5. The relay armature, however, is pulled down by a coil which is energized from the headlamp circuit. The current flows through a brown wire, through the forward limit switch and opening field, causing the armature to rotate in a direction to open the visors. When the visors are open, the motor arm depresses the forward limit switch, thereby opening the circuit.

When the visors are closed and the rear limit switch is open, the black wire will be "hot" and the brown wire will be "dead". Then the visors are open and the forward limit switch is open, the brown wire will be "hot" and the black wire will be "dead". However, if the visor linkage is misadjusted so that the rotation of the motor arm is stopped before it depresses (opens) one of the limit switches, a connection will be maintained through the motor fields so that both brown and black wires will be "hot". See steps 2 and 4 under CHECKING PROCEDURE. Therefore, if the test light lights from both wires, the limit switch at the end of that cycle is not opening, allowing a continuous drain on the battery.

-5-

1 1

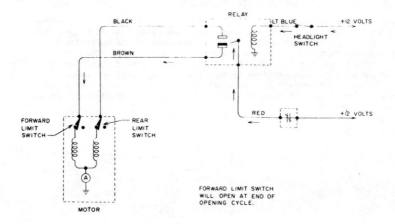

OPENING CYCLE

FIGURE 5

When a limit switch fails to open at the end of either the opening or closing cycle, the continuous current draw through the stalled visor motor soon causes a thermal circuit breaker in the armature circuit of the motor to open. Even though the motor is turned on in the opposite direction (where the load is normal), a wait of as much as 45 seconds may expected to allow time for the circuit breaker to cool and reclose.

E. J. Hresko
Manager, Technical Service

12

Date   June 25, 1964

Subject   1964 Model Riviera Door Window Glass

All 1963 model 4747 and 1964 model 4747 Riviera up to
and including body number 32810 were built using door
window glass with the glass channel and filler as an
integral part of the glass.

Therefore all 1963 Riviera models, and 1964 Riviera
models up to and including body number 32810 (approximately
mid June production) use the following door glass, channel
and filler assembly for service:

4882514 Right Glass, Filler & Channel (Clear Glass)
4882515 Left Glass, Filler & Channel (Clear Glass)
4882516 Right Glass, Filler & Channel (Soft Ray Glass)
4882517 Left Glass, Filler & Channel (Soft Ray Glass)

The 1964 model Riviera cars built after mid June with
body number 32811 and higher will use the following replacement glass:

4469077 (Right or Left) Glass (Less Filler & Channel) Clear
                                                       Glass
4469078 (Right or Left) Glass (Less Filler & Channel) Soft
                                                       Ray

The lower sash channel for the after type jobs is available
and listed group 10.685. The filler is also listed in group
10.685.

Parts and Accessories

Specifications Department

13

BUICK
DEALER SERVICE
INFORMATION

Dealer Letter No.	File Under Group No.
64-166	13-24

BUICK MOTOR DIVISION, GENERAL MOTORS CORPORATION, FLINT 2, MICHIGAN

July 3, 1964

TO ALL BUICK DEALERS

SUBJECT: Replacement Procedure for Rear Fender Ornament Grille - 1963-1964
Buick Riviera

In replacing the rear fender ornament grilles, Gr. 12.116, Parts 1396179 and
1396184, on the 1963 or 1964 Buick Riviera Style, a problem of molding stud
to quarter outer panel hole mismatch may be encountered. The forward studs
on the upper and lower grille have been moved 3/8" forward, causing the mismatch. If this condition exists, the following installation procedure is recommended.

1. Position new molding to quarter panel and lightly mark location for new
   slot.

2. Center punch two (2) small dimples in marked slot area.

3. Drill two (2) 3/32" holes at dimpled location.

4. File slot to approximately 1/8" x 1/4".

5. File and fit until stud retaining clip engages in slot.

   NOTE: Clip retention should be very snug as an oversize slot will cause
         clip to be forced through the quarter panel when grille is engaged.

6. Seal unused holes in replacement panels by cementing body tape over hole
   from inside panel. On panels with stud retaining clips still engaged at
   the unused holes, seal from outside with body caulking compound to prevent
   waterleaks.

7. Install new retaining clips in slot.

8. Position grille to panel and snap in place, starting at the rear of grille.

E. J. Hresko
Manager, Technical Service

BUICK DEALER
SERVICE
INFORMATION

Dealer Letter No.   File Under Group No.

65-25   5-5

BUICK MOTOR DIVISION   GENERAL MOTORS CORPORATION   FLINT, MICHIGAN 48550

October 9, 1964

TO ALL BUICK DEALERS

SUBJECT: Super Turbine 300 and 400 Transmission Case Porosity

Super turbine 300 and 400 transmission leaks caused by case porosity have successfully been repaired with the transmission in the car by using the following recommended procedures:

1. Road test and bring the transmission to operating temperature, approximately 170°.

2. Raise car on a hoist or jack stand, engine running, and locate source of oil leak. On super turbine 400, check for leaks with the transmission in low range 1st gear and low range 2nd gear. On super turbine 300, check for oil leaks in low, drive, and reverse.

   NOTE: Use of a mirror is helpful in finding leaks.

3. Shut engine off and thoroughly clean area to be repaired with a cleaning solvent (fabric cleaner) and a brush - air dry.

   NOTE: A clean, dry soldering acid brush can be used to clean the area and also to apply the epoxy cement.

4. Using instructions of the manufacturer, mix a sufficient amount of epoxy, Gr. No. 0.423, Part No. 1360016, to make the repair.

   NOTE: Observe cautions in handling.

5. While the transmission case is still HOT, apply the epoxy to the area to be repaired.

6 NOTE: Make certain the area to be repaired is fully covered.

6. Allow cement to cure for 3 hours before starting engine.

7. Road test and check for leaks.

E. J. Hresko
Manager, Technical Service

WGH

BUICK
DEALER SERVICE
INFORMATION

BUICK MOTOR DIVISION, GENERAL MOTORS CORPORATION, FLINT 2, MICHIGAN

September 25, 1964

TO ALL BUICK DEALERS

SUBJECT: Correct Installation of Rocker Arm Shafts -
401 and 425 Engines

As a possible cause of oil consumption, the improper installation of the rocker arm shafts is often overlooked. If
installed upside down, the rocker arm lubrication holes face
upward and allow oil to pass between the rocker arm and the
shaft. Since the oil is under pressure, it spurts into the
overhead, drains down the valve stems and into the combustion
chambers.

This illustration shows a correctly installed shaft. The
notch on the end of the shaft must be in the position shown
to properly position the lubricating holes at the bottom of
the rocker arm.

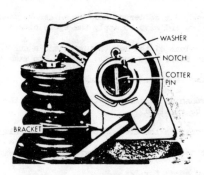

E. J. Hresko
Manager, Technical Service

WGH

16

BUICK DEALER
SERVICE
INFORMATION

Dealer Letter No.   File Under Group No.

65-97   10-18

BUICK MOTOR DIVISION   GENERAL MOTORS CORPORATION   FLINT, MICHIGAN 48550

January 29, 1965

TO ALL BUICK DEALERS

SUBJECT: Engine Idle and Timing Adjustments - 1959 Through 1965

1. Adjust contact point dwell angle to 30 degrees.

2. Adjust engine idle to specifications below.

3. Disconnect distributor vacuum hose.

4. Adjust engine timing to the following specifications:

	1959			1960	
Idle		Timing	Idle		Timing
500 RPM		12° (Auto. Trans.)	525 RPM		12° (Auto. Trans.)
500 RPM		5° (Man. Trans.)	525 RPM		5° (Man. Trans.)

	1961			1962	
525 RPM		12° (Upper Series)	525 RPM		12° (Upper Series)
525 RPM		5° (Lower Series)	525 RPM		5° (Lower Series)

	1963			1964-5	
500 RPM		12° (Upper Series AT)	550 RPM		5° (V-6 Engine)
500 RPM		5° (Upper Series MT)	550 RPM		$2\frac{1}{2}^O$ (300 Cu.In.V-8)
500 RPM		5° (Lower Series)	500 RPM		$2\frac{1}{2}^O$ (401 & 425 V-8--Exc. Dual 4-B Auto.Trans.)
			500 RPM		12° (Dual 4-B Auto.Trans.)

NOTE: If car is equipped with an air conditioner, add 50 RPM to idle specification (with air conditioner turned off). In 1963, 1964 and 1965 automatic transmission cars, adjust idle in drive range.

E. J. Hresko
Manager, Technical Service

WGH

BUICK DEALER
SERVICE
INFORMATION

Dealer Letter No.	File Under Group No.
65-140	5-14

BUICK MOTOR DIVISION   GENERAL MOTORS CORPORATION   FLINT, MICHIGAN 48550

April 2, 1965

SUBJECT: 1964-65 Super Turbine 400 Transmission "Clunk"

A few dealer product reports have been received referring to a "clunk" in some 1964-65 Super Turbine 400 transmissions. This condition will occur when the throttle is released suddenly with the transmission in third gear.

In many instances, complaints of the above nature have been corrected using the following procedures:

1. Dash pot adjustment. Adjust the dash pot with the engine at normal operating temperature and with idle speed and mixture correctly adjusted.

    a. While observing dash pot, open carburetor and allow throttle to snap closed. If dash pot does not delay closing action just before throttle is closed, adjust dash pot for more interference. If return to idle drags out excessively (more than two seconds), adjust dash pot for less interference.

    b. As a final check, hold car with brakes and put transmission in drive, then jab accelerator pedal. If car stalls, adjust dash pot for slightly more interference and recheck as necessary.

    c. Tighten lock nut securely.

At first glance, there may be some doubt as to what the correct dash pot adjustment has to do with a "clunk" condition. If the dash pot was misadjusted so that it was not contacting the throttle lever at curb idle position, this would allow the throttle to go back to curb idle without the advantage of the cushion offered by the dash pot. Without this cushion, a big torque change is experienced from a driving RPM to curb idle. This big torque change will cause the "clunk" condition. If the dash pot is correctly adjusted, the throttle lever will contact the dash pot and the throttle will be cushioned back to curb idle.

2. If the dash pot adjustment is found to be correct, then lubricate the splines between the transmission output shaft and the propeller shaft front slip yoke. It is recommended that wheel bearing grease be used.

3. In addition to the above, if necessary, apply wheel bearing lubricant between the crankshaft pilot bore and converter hub.

E. J. Hresko
Manager, Technical Service

DEC

CHAPTER TWO

1965 RIVIERA

BUICK DEALER
SERVICE
INFORMATION

BUICK
Authorized
Service

Dealer Letter No.   File Under Group No.

65-33   2-2

BUICK MOTOR DIVISION GENERAL MOTORS CORPORATION FLINT, MICHIGAN 48550

October 23, 1964

TO ALL BUICK DEALERS

SUBJECT: 1965 Buick Engine Identification and Foreign Travel
Information

Listed on the reverse side are the various engines used in the
1965 Buick automobiles.

Owners contemplating travel outside the United States should
be cautioned to check on the quality of fuel available before their
trip. For your convenience, the engine chart will serve as a
guide in determining engine identification, compression ratio,
fuel octane requirements, etc. Zone Service Managers have a
publication listing the octanes of the fuels found in most countries of the world.

If satisfactory fuels cannot be assured, the compression ratio
should be lowered by installing lower compression ratio pistons
as indicated on the chart.

NOTE: Engine damage caused by detonation as a result of the
use of low octane fuels is not considered a defect in
material or workmanship; therefore, cannot be considered for warranty adjustment.

E. J. Hresko
Manager, Technical Service

WGH

Engine Mfg. Code No. Prefix	Series	Engine Description and Carburetor Equipment	Compression Ratio	Octane Requirement	Horsepower at RPM	Piston and Pin Part No.
LH	43-44	225 cu. in. V-6 - 1 barrel	9.0 to 1	85 Motor 93 Research	155 at 4400	1399524
LK	43-44	225 cu. in. V-6 - 1 barrel (export low compression)	7.6 to 1	74 Motor 83 Research	140 at 4400	1399610
LL	43-44-45	300 cu. in. V-8 - 2 barrel	9.0 to 1	85 Motor 93 Research	210 at 4400	1399524
LM	43-44-45	300 cu. in. V-8 - 2 barrel (export low compression)	7.6 to 1	74 Motor 83 Research	195 at 4600	1399610
LP	43-44-45	300 cu. in. V-8 - 4 barrel	10.25 to 1	90 Motor 99 Research	250 at 4800	1399525
LT	46-48-49	401 cu. in. V-8 - 4 barrel	10.25 to 1	90 Motor 99 Research	325 at 4400	1388538
LV	46-48-49	401 cu. in. V-8 - 4 barrel (export low compression)	8.75 to 1	85 Motor 93 Research	315 at 4400	1388539
LW	46-48-49	425 cu. in. V-8 - 4 barrel	10.25 to 1	90 Motor 99 Research	340 at 4400	1399211
LX	46-48-49	425 cu. in. V-8 - 2-4 barrel	10.25 to 1	90 Motor 99 Research	360 at 4400	1399211

Date   April 1, 1965

Subject   Skylark and Riviera Series <u>Gran Sport Option</u>

<u>The following is information which pertains to method of cataloguing parts used in the Gran Sport Option.</u>

For 1965, the following models may have the Gran Sport Option:

4427 - 4437 - 4467 - 9447

If a particular part is specific to the Gran Sport Option, it will be so identified in the 1965 Parts Catalog. The following are examples of the identifications peculiar to the Gran Sport Option.

0.027 - <u>400 Engine</u> - 1372540 - Pad, Engine Mounting
        (Skylark Series Gran Sport option has 400 Cubic
        Inch Engine)

8.130 - <u>4000 Gran Sport</u> - 137-988-989 - Fender, Front
        (Skylark Gran Sport)
8.147 - <u>Riviera Gran Sport</u> - 1365758 - Monogram

If the part is used on all Special Series (Including Skylark) or the Riviera Series, with or without the Gran Sport Option, there will be no reference made to the Gran Sport Option.
For Example: Group 8.000 - Special - 1361752 - Hood
              Group 8.000 - Riviera - 1365114 - Hood

Therefore the above hoods are used on their specific models regardless if the car is equipped with the Gran Sport Option or not.

Parts and Accessories

Specifications Department

BUICK DEALER
SERVICE
INFORMATION

Dealer Letter No.	File Under Group No.
65-101A	6-5

BUICK MOTOR DIVISION   GENERAL MOTORS CORPORATION   FLINT, MICHIGAN 48550

June 11, 1965

TO ALL BUICK DEALERS

SUBJECT: 1965 Gear Ratios, Speedometer Gears
and Gear Adapters

SUPERCEDES DEALER LETTER 65-101, DATED
FEBRUARY 12, 1965

Attached are charts indicating 1965 gear ratios
and corresponding speedometer gears used on the
various models with the different transmission
and tire options.

This is merely for your information if such
should be needed.

E. J. Hresko
Manager, Technical Service

1965 - 46-48-49000

AXLE RATIO	TRANSMISSION ASM.		SPEEDO DRIVING WORM	SPEEDO DRIVEN GEAR			TIRE SIZE	DRIVEN GEAR ADAPTER
	TYPE	MODEL CODE	N° OF TEETH	N° OF TEETH	IDENTIFYING COLOR		SIZE	
2.78	AUTOMATIC	BJ,BN,BQ	19	39	BROWN		8.15 X 15	
			19	38	BLUE		8.45 X 15	
			19	38	BLUE		8.85 X 15	
	3 & 4 - SPEED SYNCHROMESH	(3-SP)KB	9	18	BROWN		8.15 X 15	
			9	18	BROWN		8.45 X 15	
		(4-SP)KS	9	18	BROWN		8.85 X 15	
3.07	AUTOMATIC	BJ,BN,BQ	19	43	PURPLE		8.15 X 15	
			19	42	GREEN		8.45 X 15	
			19	41	YELLOW		8.85 X 15	
	3 & 4 - SPEED SYNCHROMESH	(3-SP)KA (4-SP)KT	8	18	BROWN		8.15 X 15	
			9	20	BLUE		8.45 X 15	
		(3-SP)KB (4-SP)KS	9	19	NATURAL		8.85 X 15	
3.23	AUTOMATIC	BR, BT	17	40	BLACK		8.15 X 15	
			17	40	BLACK		8.45 X 15	
			17	39	BROWN		8.85 X 15	
	3 & 4 - SPEED SYNCHROMESH	(3 SP)KA (4 SP)KT	8	19	NATURAL		8.15 X 15	
		(3 SP)KB (4 SP)KS	9	21	RED		8.45 X 15	
		(3 SP)KA (4 SP)KT	8	18	BROWN		8.85 X 15	
3.36	AUTOMATIC	BR, BT	17	42	GREEN		8.15 X 15	
			17	41	YELLOW		8.45 X 15	
			17	40	BLACK		8.85 X 15	
	3 & 4 - SPEED SYNCHROMESH	(3-SP)KA	8	20	BLUE		8.15 X 15	
			8	19	NATURAL		8.45 X 15	
		(4-SP)KT	8	19	NATURAL		8.85 X 15	
3.42	AUTOMATIC	BR, BS, BT	17	43	PURPLE		8.15 X 15	
			17	42	GREEN		8.45 X 15	
			17	41	YELLOW		8.85 X 15	
	3 & 4 - SPEED SYNCHROMESH	(3-SP)KA	8	20	BLUE		8.15 X 15	
			8	20	BLUE		8.45 X 15	
		(4-SP)KT	8	19	NATURAL		8.85 X 15	
3.58	AUTOMATIC	BJ, BN, BQ	19	43	PURPLE		8.15 X 15	
			19	42	GREEN		8.45 X 15	9775436
			19	41	YELLOW		8.85 X 15	
	3 & 4 - SPEED SYNCHROMESH	(3-SP)KA (4-SP)KT	8	21	RED		8.15 X 15	
			7	18	BROWN		8.45 X 15	
		(3-SP)KC (4-SP)KR	7	18	BROWN		8.85 X 15	
3.91	AUTOMATIC	BJ, BN, BQ	19	40	BLACK		8.15 X 15	
			19	39	BROWN		8.45 X 15	1367644
			19	39	BROWN		8.85 X 15	
	3 & 4 - SPEED SYNCHROMESH	(3-SP)KC	7	20	BLUE		8.15 X 15	
			7	20	BLUE		8.45 X 15	
		(4-SP)KR	7	19	NATURAL		8.85 X 15	
4.45	AUTOMATIC							
	3 & 4 - SPEED SYNCHROMESH	(3-SP)KD	6	20	BLUE		8.15 X 15	
			6	19	NATURAL		8.45 X 15	
		(4-SP)KP	6	19	NATURAL		8.85 X 15	

TO Zone Service Managers   **DATE** October 20, 1965
      Zone Managers
      Asst. General Sales Managers
      Regional Managers
      Internal List

SUBJECT Perma Anti-Skid Control

Inquiries have been received from time to time by General Motors
divisions and field personnel from individuals and dealers relative
to the use of a product called "Perma Anti-Skid Control" on General
Motors vehicles. This unit, developed by Perma Research and Development Company and now manufactured by Singer Company, is a braking effort
sensing device which, according to the manufacturer, provides straight,
smooth, controlled stopping regardless of the condition of the road
surface.

General Motors engineers have evaluated the effects of the installation and operation of the "Perma Anti-Skid Control" on General
Motors vehicles. We have been advised that the operation of the
"Perma Anti-Skid Control" has some adverse effects upon the normal
operation of the vehicle's braking system and may very well have a
detrimental effect upon a number of mechanical components and parts
of the vehicle.

Moreover, the operation of the device may result in discomfort to the
driver or other vehicle occupants.

The use of the "Perma Anti-Skid Control" on Buick motor vehicles is
neither recommended nor approved.

Questions may nevertheless be directed to zone personnel regarding the
effect of an existing or proposed "Perma Anti-Skid Control" installation
upon the application of the unexpired portion of the Manufacturer's New
Vehicle Warranty. Replies to all such inquiries should be consistent
with the following statement, which applies as well to all other products
not manufactured or supplied by General Motors (whether installed on
the vehicle at a Buick dealership or elsewhere):

> "The General Motors New Vehicle Warranty applies to the new
> vehicle and to all equipment and accessories thereon which are
> manufactured or supplied by General Motors. On the other hand,

products not manufactured or supplied by General Motors are
not covered by the General Motors New Vehicle Warranty. The
applicability or non-applicability of any unexpired portion
of the New Vehicle Warranty following the installation of such
product would depend upon the extent to which such product
adversely affected the performance or reliability of the vehicle
or any of its parts or components. However, any defects in
material or workmanship on parts or components that are not
affected by such product would be processed under said Warranty;
approval of such warranty claims, based on the repair or replacement of such unaffected parts or components, would not be refused
simply because a product not manufactured or supplied by General
Motors had been installed on the particular vehicle."

Thomas Ploucha
Asst. General Service Mgr.

WGH:dm

Dealer P&A Bulletin

Date   October 16, 1964

Subject   **New Accessories for 1965**
981051 - Foot Control Switch for Wonderbar Radio
981019 - Cornering Lamp Switch

Two new switches are offered as 1965 accessories.

The Wonderbar Radio Foot Control Switch is offered as a separate item this year. It is no longer a standard part of the Wonderbar Radio. However, some Wonderbar customers may desire this feature. The switch package is available for such owners. It is described as follows:

Group Number	Part Number	Description	Dealer Cost	Sugg. List
9.642	981051	Foot Control Switch (Wonderbar Radio)	$1.80	$3.00

The Cornering Lamp Switch offers manual control of the Cornering Lamps. Both lamps are lighted when the switch, located to the left of the steering column on the lower instrument panel, is actuated. The switch overrides the directional signal switch.

This control offers the use of the Cornering Lamps as additional driving aids on narrow drives or roads and in foggy, rainy or snowy weather, in helping to locate the center line and/or the road edge.

The switch is described as follows:

Group Number	Part Number	Description	Dealer Cost	Sugg. List
2.585	981019	Cornering Lamp Switch	$4.80	$8.00

You may use the attached order form for your initial requirements.

Parts and Accessories

Merchandising Department

27

BUICK DEALER
SERVICE
INFORMATION

Dealer Letter No.	File Under Group No.
65-43	11-2

BUICK MOTOR DIVISION   GENERAL MOTORS CORPORATION   FLINT, MICHIGAN 48550

October 30, 1964

TO ALL BUICK DEALERS

SUBJECT: Use of Air Conditioner Compressor With a Larger Diameter Pulley
On Gran Sport Riviera's - 1965 Models

The air conditioner compressor on all Gran Sport Riviera's will be equipped
with a 5 inch diameter pulley instead of the normally provided 4.72 inch
diameter pulley. Because of the higher engine RPM's on the Gran Sport
Series, a larger diameter pulley is required to maintain the compressor
RPM's within safe limitations.

E. J. Hresko
Manager, Technical Service

WGH

Dealer P&A Bulletin

DATE: November 1, 1965

SUBJECT: Guide-Matic and Twilight Sentinel Dealer Installation Packages
          for 1966 LeSabre, Wildcat, Electra and Riviera Models

Here is an excellent opportunity to gain extra sales and profits from two popular
accessories -- Guide-Matic Headlamp Control and Twilight Sentinel. Both of these
profitable accessories are now available to Buick customers only as Dealer Installed
Accessories, which gives you an exclusive opportunity to increase your accessory
sales.

Guide-Matic Headlamp Control, the device which senses on-coming headlights and
automatically controls the dimming of headlamps on the car on which it is installed,
has been, for the past several years, a "must" for many Buick owners.

Twilight Sentinel will turn headlamps on automatically at dusk or on storm darkened
days and turn them off again when sufficient daylight returns. For added convenience
the Twilight Sentinel will cause the headlamps to be left on for a short time to
provide a path of light for the driver and passengers as they leave the car at night.

Both accessories can be easily and quickly installed by merely plugging into existing wiring harness -- no wire splicing or soldering. These accessories have been
developed exclusively for Buick.

Guide-Matic Headlamp Control and Twilight Sentinel will be available December 1,
1965. Both units will be shipped direct from our supplier to dealers. All orders
are to be forwarded to the Buick Motor Division Accessory Department, Flint, Mich.

Accessory numbers for the packages, prices and flat rate time are as follows:

GUIDE-MATIC HEADLAMP CONTROL

Group Number	Part Number	Model Application	List Price	Dealer Price	Flat Rate
2.459	981181	5000-6000 8000-9000	$45.00	$33.75	1.5 hrs.

TWILIGHT SENTINEL

Group Number	Part Number	Model Application	List Price	Dealer Price	Flat Rate	
2.485	981182	5000-6000 8000-9000	$35.00	$26.25	5000-6000-8000 9000	1 hr. 2 hr.

Use the attached order form and order now!   Your new car customers will want
them.   Your new car salesmen can sell them.

Parts and Accessories

Merchandising Department

BUICK DEALER
SERVICE
INFORMATION

Dealer Letter No.   File Under Group No.

65-36   3-3

BUICK MOTOR DIVISION   GENERAL MOTORS CORPORATION   FLINT, MICHIGAN 48550

October 16, 1964

TO ALL BUICK DEALERS

SUBJECT: First Start Stalls - Carter 4-Barrel Carburetors

Complaints have been received of hard starting of Carter carburetor equipped
cars. This trouble generally occurs after the car was parked hot and left
standing 12 hours or more. The engine starts briefly, but stalls immediately
and then must be cranked for some time before it fires again.

A possible cause of the trouble is gasoline evaporation from the carburetor
resulting in a low fuel level in the float bowl. However, if the carburetor
is adjusted carefully to specifications and is operating properly, fuel should
pick up from the bottom of the float bowl and the engine should keep running or,
at the worst, re-start rapidly and keep running on the second start.

To minimize first start stalls, check the following adjustments:

1.   Choke Adjustment - Index is specified on all except 300 engine automatic
     transmission cars (1 notch rich). Make sure choke valve is perfectly free
     and closes fully. (Rule of thumb, choke should be barely closed at 80^0
     and proportionately tighter at colder temperatures.) For repeat complaints,
     adjust choke 1 or 2 notches richer; never go over 2 notches or cold weather
     flooding will result.

2.   Choke Piston Adjustment - Make sure the choke valve is not open too much
     when the choke piston reaches the "vacuum break" slot in the bore. (This
     is the position the choke piston and valve assume immediately after starting.)
     See 1965 Buick Service Manuals for adjustments; lower series - Figure 3-53,
     upper series - Figure 3-76.

3.   Fast Idle Cam Adjustment - Make sure the fast idle cam rotates fully to
     its index mark when the choke valve is closed. (If fast idle screw is
     below index mark, fast idle speed will be too slow for all choke positions.)
     For lower series - see Figure 3-55; for upper series - see Figure 3-78.

4.   Fast Idle Adjustment - Make sure the fast idle speed is not too slow.
     Specification is 600 RPM in drive on lowest step of cam. (A too slow adjust-
     ment here will result in too little throttle opening on starting step of
     cam.)

Since a first start stall is the result of running out of fuel, pumping the
accelerator will hasten the restart.

E. J. Hfesko
Manager, Technical Service

WGH

BUICK DEALER
SERVICE
INFORMATION

BUICK Authorized Service

Dealer Letter No. 65-127

File Under Group No. 3-9

BUICK MOTOR DIVISION GENERAL MOTORS CORPORATION FLINT, MICHIGAN 48550

March 12, 1965

TO ALL BUICK DEALERS

SUBJECT: Linkage Sticking - Dual 4-Barrel Carburetor Engines

If a complaint is received that the throttle linkage sticks or binds
in a car equipped with dual 4-barrel carburetors, remove the air
cleaner and operate the throttle linkage by hand to determine the
point where the sticking originates. If you find that the bolt is
sticking where it slides through the front carburetor trunnion, replace the solid trunnion with a new open trunnion. See the illustration for identification of the new trunnion.

Order Group 3.430 - Part 1375060 - Trunnion

Before assembling the new trunnion, make sure the bolt and the trunnion are clean and dry. Just as carburetor linkage should never be
oiled, throttle linkage, also, should never be oiled. Oil would only
become gummy and collect dust and dirt. Lubricate only at points
marked "L" using Lubriplate or a good chassis grease.

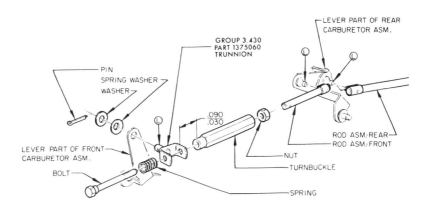

E. J. Hresko
Manager, Technical Service

CEB

31

BUICK DEALER
SERVICE
INFORMATION

Dealer Letter No.	File Under Group No.
65-129	3-10

BUICK MOTOR DIVISION   GENERAL MOTORS CORPORATION   FLINT, MICHIGAN 48550

March 12, 1965

TO ALL BUICK DEALERS

SUBJECT: Hard Starting Due to Choke Sticking Open 1964-1965 Carter 4-Barrel Carburetors

When hard cold starting is found to be caused by the choke valve sticking open, the next step is to determine the exact location of the bind in the choke mechanism.

Trace location of bind as follows:

1. Remove air cleaner. Remove choke cover, gasket and baffle plate.

2. Hold throttle open to clear fast idle cam. Close choke valve with finger and release; choke valve should fall open from its own weight.

3. If choke will not fall open, next disconnect upper end of rod to fast idle cam; also disconnect upper end of rod to choke piston housing. Again see if choke valve will fall open; if not, choke valve and shaft must be disassembled for a thorough cleaning.

4. Next, see if fast idle cam mechanism will fall from its own weight. If not, this mechanism must be cleaned thoroughly. These parts, like all of the choke mechanism, must be assembled without lubrication.

5. Last, see if choke piston mechanism will allow piston to drop to bottom of bore from its own weight. If not, remove choke piston housing assembly, disassemble and clean thoroughly. If parts do not free-up, we are recommending replacement of the complete choke piston, linkage and housing assembly with a new service package.

The reason for recommending this replacement - some choke piston housings have been found with blisters in the bore; also some piston linkages have been found with binding rivets. The new service package listed below will provide a more positive and permanent correction for a choke which is sticking due to either of these two defects.

Order Choke Piston, Linkage and Housing Packages as follows:

Group	Part No.	Application	Carb. Nos.	Dealer Net
3.750	1376099	1964-65 All Dual 4-bbl.	3634S-3646S-3924S-3925S	3.60
3.750	1376100	1964-401 & 425 Eng., All Trans. 1965-401 & 425 Eng., Man Trans.	3633S-3635S-3665S-3922S	3.60
3.750	1376101	1965-401 & 425 Eng., Auto Trans.	3921S-3923S	3.60
3.750	1376102	1965-300 Eng., All Trans.	3826S-3827S	3.00

Install package as follows:

1. Remove old choke piston, linkage and housing assembly and install new package. This can be done on the car. Make sure small round rubber gasket (from package) is installed in new piston housing.

2. Install all linkage. Make choke piston linkage adjustment as outlined in the Buick Chassis Service Manual which applies.

3. Install baffle plate, new gasket and thermostatic coil assembly. Set choke per specifications. Connect choke heat tube to housing.

4. Set idle speed and mixture as described in service manual. Adjust fast idle at 600 RPM with engine at normal operating temperature, transmission in drive, and fast idle screw on lowest step of cam.

Flat Rate Time for installation of the package is .4 hour including adjustments. Dealer Net Price is shown above.

We are requesting that you return any defective choke housing assemblies along with the green "Parts Inspection Copy" of the AFA in Envelope S-728-1. Ship by parcel post to the following address:

> Buick Motor Division
> General Motors Corporation
> Clear Signal Area
> Factory 02
> Flint, Michigan - 48550

E. J. Hresko
Manager, Technical Service

BUICK
DEALER SERVICE
INFORMATION

Dealer Letter No.	File Under Group No.
65-5	3-1

BUICK MOTOR DIVISION, GENERAL MOTORS CORPORATION, FLINT 2, MICHIGAN

September 14, 1964

TO ALL BUICK DEALERS

SUBJECT: Throttle Rod Adjustment — 1965 All Series

To obtain proper accelerator pedal position (65^0 from horizontal — Upper Series, or 67^0 from horizontal — Lower Series) the simplest adjustment is by means of a measurement from the upper end of the throttle operating lever horizontally to the front of the dash.

Adjust Upper Series cars as shown below and Lower Series cars as shown on the reverse side of this bulletin.

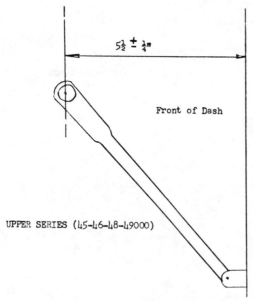

$5\frac{1}{2} \pm \frac{1}{4}''$

Front of Dash

UPPER SERIES (45-46-48-49000)

Pedal

Horizontal

Position throttle operating lever from front of dash as shown.

With carburetor at hot curb idle position, adjust throttle rod length to obtain free assembly of clevis pin thru bushings in upper end of throttle operating lever.

E. J. Hresko
Manager, Technical Service

34

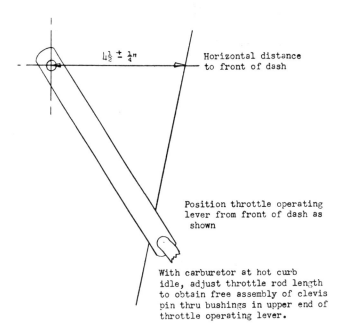

$4\frac{1}{2} \pm \frac{1}{4}"$

Horizontal distance
to front of dash

Position throttle operating
lever from front of dash as
shown

With carburetor at hot curb
idle, adjust throttle rod length
to obtain free assembly of clevis
pin thru bushings in upper end of
throttle operating lever.

BUICK DEALER SERVICE INFORMATION

BUICK
Authorized
Service

Dealer Letter No.	File Under Group No.
65-126	3-8

BUICK MOTOR DIVISION   GENERAL MOTORS CORPORATION   FLINT, MICHIGAN 48550

March 5, 1965

TO ALL BUICK DEALERS

SUBJECT: Hot Surge Complaints - Carter 4-Barrel Carburetors

Under extremely hot operating conditions, you may get a complaint of a surge condition on a Carter 4-barrel carburetor equipped car. This surge, which is most
pronounced at 35 to 40 MPH, occurs for a short time after restarting a very hot
engine. In this case, surge is due to excessive heat in the float bowl causing
violent boiling of the fuel. Instead of mixing solid fuel with air, the carburetor mixes fuel and vapor with air, resulting in a lean mixture to the engine.

A new carburetor to intake manifold gasket has been released which will help reduce this problem. This new gasket, which contains an insulating material, was
installed in all 4-barrel carburetor equipped Buicks built after February 22, 1965.

If insulated gaskets are needed for a field fix of complaint cars, order Group
3.726 - Part #1375460 - Gasket.

Too much heat in the float bowl can also result in a slow start complaint; this
is because an engine which is shut off while very hot may cause boil-off of most
of the volatile (quick-starting) part of the fuel in the float bowl. The remaining
low level of non-volatile fuel will result in slow starting. The new insulated
gasket may help to reduce this type of complaint.

The new gasket is black with a smooth consistency all the way through; the old
gasket is gray with a steel-asbestos mesh construction. To determine which gasket
is installed on a certain car, remove the air cleaner and scrape the edge of the
gasket with a sharp cornered screwdriver. If the gasket is of the early steel-
asbestos type, scraping will expose fine steel wires.

Flat Rate Time for replacing the gasket, including idle speed, mixture and fast
idle adjustments, is .7 hr.

E. J. Hresko
Manager, Technical Service

WGH

BUICK DEALER
SERVICE
INFORMATION

Dealer Letter No.		File Under Group No.
65-151		5-17

BUICK MOTOR DIVISION GENERAL MOTORS CORPORATION FLINT, MICHIGAN 48550

April 23, 1965

TO ALL BUICK DEALERS

SUBJECT: Super Turbine 300 and 400 Transmission Oil Checking Procedure

Before diagnosis of any transmission complaint is attempted, there must be an understanding of oil checking procedures and what appearance the oil should have. Many times a transmission malfunction can be traced to low oil level, improper reading of dipstick, or oil appearance; therefore, a careful analysis of the condition of oil and the level may eliminate needless repairs.

When checking oil level in the Super Turbine 300 or 400 transmission, the following procedure should be observed to obtain the most accurate reading:

1. Bring transmission oil to operating temperature of 170°F. Usually driving five (5) miles with frequent stops and starts will bring the transmission to operating temperature. Before oil is checked the selector lever should be moved through all driving ranges.

   NOTE: Prior to road testing car, oil level must be visible on dipstick.

2. Oil level must be checked with the selector lever in Park (P) or Neutral (N) position ONLY, engine running, and the vehicle on LEVEL pavement.

   NOTE: If oil level is checked in any other driving range, a lower reading will result.

3. Dipstick should always be inserted into the oil filler tube so that the oil level indicator markings are toward the center of the car.

Also, when the dipstick is removed, it should be noted whether the oil is devoid of air bubbles or not. Oil with air bubbles gives an indication of an oil leak in the suction lines, which can cause erratic operation and slippage. Water in the oil imparts a milky, pink cast to the oil and can cause "spewing".

E. J. Hresko
Manager, Technical Service

BUICK DEALER
SERVICE
INFORMATION

Dealer Letter No. File Under Group No.

65-67   2-3

BUICK MOTOR DIVISION   GENERAL MOTORS CORPORATION   FLINT, MICHIGAN 48550

December 11, 1964

TO ALL BUICK DEALERS

SUBJECT: Discontinuance of Valve Stem Seals 1965 - 401 and 425 Engines

Since the beginning of 1965 production, all 401 and 425 engines have been
equipped with lead-coated valve stem keys and valve stem seals. The addition of these items greatly improved oil economy by preventing the flow of
oil along the valve stems. However, recent tests conducted by the Engineering
Department have shown that the seals are unnecessary when the lead-coated
keys are used. Therefore, all engines built after approximately December 1,
1964, will be assembled without valve stem seals.

E. J. Hresko
Manager, Technical Service

WGH

BUICK DEALER
SERVICE
INFORMATION

Dealer Letter No.　　File Under Group No.

65-21　　　　5-2

BUICK MOTOR DIVISION   GENERAL MOTORS CORPORATION   FLINT, MICHIGAN 48550

October 2, 1964

TO ALL BUICK DEALERS

SUBJECT: Transmission Oil Leak At Breather Pipe - Super Turbine
          400 Transmission

There have been several cases reported of transmission oil coming
out of the breather pipe on super turbine 400 transmissions. Due
to the difficulty in properly diagnosing the cause of the leak, the
following possibilities are listed:

1. Transmission oil level to high

2. Strainer "O" ring cut

3. Strainer intake pipe improperly welded

4. Case porosity above intake pipe "O" ring seal

    NOTE: The above defects will cause the transmission oil to aer-
           ate (foam). This can be seen on the dipstick in the form
           of small bubbles.

5. Pump to case gasket mispositioned

6. Porosity in case at the outer edge of the pump mounting pad that
    may go through the cooler hoses

7. Chip or dirt between pump cover and pump body

E. J. Hresko
Manager, Technical Service

BUICK DEALER
SERVICE
INFORMATION

Dealer Letter No.	File Under Group No.
65-35	5-7

BUICK MOTOR DIVISION   GENERAL MOTORS CORPORATION   FLINT, MICHIGAN 48550

October 16, 1964

TO ALL BUICK DEALERS

SUBJECT: 1965 Super Turbine 400 Automatic Transmission L^2 and L^1 Ranges

To aid the new car salesman and the service salesman in further understanding the L^2 and L^1 ranges in the Super Turbine 400 transmission, the following information is being published:

The 1965 Super Turbine 400 transmission has been designed for greater driving flexibility. Instead of just one Low range, as used in 1964, we now have two low ranges, L^2 and L^1.

The most frequent use of these two new low ranges would be for braking down long, steep grades. The choice of which low range should be used would depend upon the severity of the grade.

If traveling down a moderate grade, and it is desired to have a slight braking action without applying the brakes, move the transmission selector into L^2 position. When the selector lever is moved from D to L^2 the transmission shifts into second gear. The transmission will remain in second gear until the car reaches a speed of 10 MPH, when it will shift into first gear. Under no circumstance will the transmission again up-shift into **direct** Drive while the selector lever is in L^2 range.

If traveling down a severe grade, and it is desired to have maximum braking from the transmission, move the transmission selector lever into L^1 position. When the selector lever is moved from D to L^1 at speeds above 45 MPH the transmission will down-shift into second gear. When slowing down to a speed of approximately 45 MPH, the transmission will shift into first gear giving maximum transmission braking. Automatic up-shift will not occur while the selector lever is in L^1 position. The transmission selector lever must be put into Drive range before the transmission will again up-shift into **direct** Drive.

WM McCrocklin
W. M. McCrocklin
General Service Manager

BUICK DEALER
SERVICE
INFORMATION

Dealer Letter No.	File Under Group No.
65-112	6-6

BUICK MOTOR DIVISION   GENERAL MOTORS CORPORATION   FLINT, MICHIGAN 48550

February 19, 1965

TO ALL BUICK DEALERS

SUBJECT: Rear Axle Failures Due to Loss of Lubricant -
All 1964-1965 Models

Failure on the part of some dealers to securely tighten rear axle filler plugs during New Car Pre-Delivery Service is resulting in an increasing number of axle failures due to loss of lubricant. Failure to perform this simple check can destroy not only the rear axle, but customer satisfaction as well.

The New Car Pre-Delivery Schedule specifically states that axle lubricant level should be checked and brought to the proper level if necessary. At this time, the filler plug should be tightened to the recommended torque of 30 ft. lbs.

Because this check is a dealer responsibility, AFA's will not be accepted for failed rear axles caused by insufficient lubricant due to dealer not checking level, or to a missing or loose filler plug, unless the failure occurred prior to New Car Pre-Delivery Service.

W. M. McCrocklin
General Service Manager

EJH:dm

BUICK DEALER
SERVICE
INFORMATION

BUICK

Authorized Service

Dealer Letter No. 65-187

File Under Group No. 8-4

BUICK MOTOR DIVISION   GENERAL MOTORS CORPORATION   FLINT, MICHIGAN 48550

August 20, 1965

TO ALL BUICK DEALERS

SUBJECT: Power Steering "Squawk"

Starting with the following car serial numbers, 1965 models
equipped with power steering gear have an improved rotary
valve which eliminates a gear squawk problem encountered
while turning the steering wheel. Reliability tests demon-
strate that the new rotary valve is an effective correction
for this particular type complaint.

Breakpoints:

	LeSabre	Wildcat	Electra	Riviera
Flint	5H134000	5H912000	5H151000	5H912000
Southgate	5C106000	5C107000		
K.C., K.	5X113000	5X118000		
Wilmington	5Y114000	5Y116000		
Atlanta	5D106000	5D108000		

Many cases investigated at local dealerships revealed that
there is a tendency for dealership personnel to replace the
gear rotary valve in an attempt to correct noises not associ-
ated with this valve. For example, a moan type noise in many
cases can be greatly reduced by merely repositioning the
steering column and/or eliminating a binding steering shaft
flexible coupling. This type moan noise is much longer in
duration than the brief squawk type noise caused by the rotary
valve.

In view of the above, effective immediately, AFAs will not be
acceptable without zone authorization for rotary valve replacement on cars having serial numbers higher than those listed in
this letter.

W. M. McCrocklin
General Service Manager

BUICK DEALER
SERVICE
INFORMATION

BUICK
Authorized
Service

Dealer Letter No.

65-73

File Under Group No.

13-13

BUICK MOTOR DIVISION   GENERAL MOTORS CORPORATION   FLINT, MICHIGAN 48550

December 18, 1964

TO ALL BUICK DEALERS

SUBJECT: Intermittent Power Window Operation — 1965 Models

If intermittent operation power windows are encountered on 1965 body
styles, one of the causes may be due to an insufficient electrical
ground between the door and the body. When this condition is encountered
a ground wire should be installed between the door hinge pillar and
the body hinge pillar. One recommended location for attachment is
illustrated in Figure 1; however, if another location is desired, precautions should be taken to prevent the ground wire from being pinched
or chaffed when the door is operated.

On styles where screws retain the wiring conduit on the door hinge
pillar, the ground wire may be inserted under the rubber lip and screw
for grounding.

A ground wire may be made as shown in Figure 2.

E. J. Hresko
Manager, Technical Service

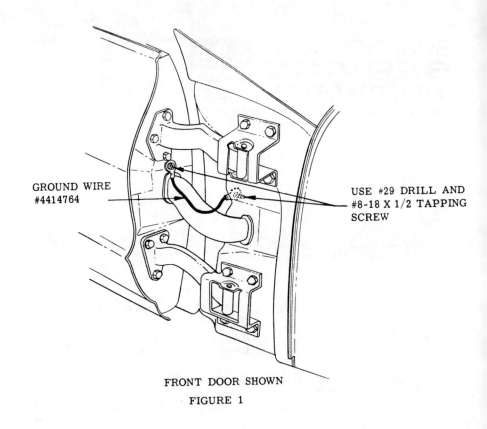

GROUND WIRE #4414764

USE #29 DRILL AND #8-18 X 1/2 TAPPING SCREW

FRONT DOOR SHOWN

FIGURE 1

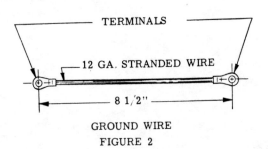

TERMINALS

12 GA. STRANDED WIRE

8 1/2"

GROUND WIRE

FIGURE 2

BUICK DEALER
SERVICE
INFORMATION

BUICK
Authorized Service

Dealer Letter No. 65-63

File Under Group No. 10-13

BUICK MOTOR DIVISION GENERAL MOTORS CORPORATION FLINT, MICHIGAN 48550

December 11, 1964

TO ALL BUICK DEALERS

SUBJECT: Manual Operation of Riviera Headlamp Visors

If the headlamp visors will not open when the lights are turned on, leave the lights on a minute to allow time for the visor motor circuit breaker to close. Since repairs cannot always be made on the spot, it is very important for every Buick mechanic to know how to manually operate headlamp visors, so the car can be driven until repairs <u>can</u> be made.

In an emergency, headlamp visors can be operated manually as follows:

1. Open hood. Reach down in back of grille and grasp right and left horizontal links firmly as close to visor motor as possible.

2. Jerk straight up on each horizontal link to snap socket in link from ball stud on motor arm.

3. Support horizontal links and manually open visors, one at a time. If car is liable to be operated some time before repairs can be made, it is advisable to tie or wire horizontal links to grille, so that they cannot rattle.

E. J. Hresko
Manager, Technical Service

WGH

45

BUICK DEALER
SERVICE
INFORMATION

BUICK MOTOR DIVISION   GENERAL MOTORS CORPORATION   FLINT, MICHIGAN 48550

Dealer Letter No.	File Under Group No.
65-26	10-3

October 9, 1964

TO ALL BUICK DEALERS

SUBJECT: Headlamp Visor Relay - 1965 Rivieras

Some cases of inoperative headlamp visors have been traced to defective relays. These relays became defective because they were mounted base upward so that water was trapped and leaked into the relay. All early-built 1965 Rivieras should be checked to see if the relays are incorrectly mounted with the base upward. See upper part of illustration. Any incorrectly mounted relays must be rotated as shown in the lower part of the illustration.

An inoperative visor relay can be detected by piercing the visor motor wires, one at a time. One wire should be "hot" with the headlamps on; the other wire should be "hot" with the headlamps off. If the same wire stays "hot" regardless of whether the headlamps are on or off, the relay is not operating. Make certain the light blue wire (relay actuating circuit) is "hot" with headlights on and "dead" with the headlights off; if relay still does not operate, install a new relay.

E. J. Hresko
Manager, Technical Service

46

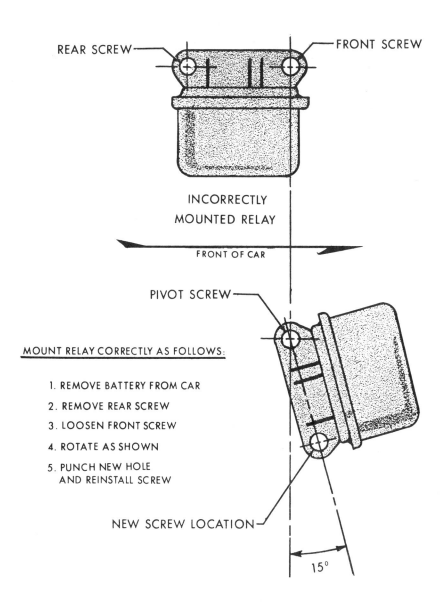

REAR SCREW — — FRONT SCREW

INCORRECTLY
MOUNTED RELAY

FRONT OF CAR

PIVOT SCREW —

MOUNT RELAY CORRECTLY AS FOLLOWS:

1. REMOVE BATTERY FROM CAR

2. REMOVE REAR SCREW

3. LOOSEN FRONT SCREW

4. ROTATE AS SHOWN

5. PUNCH NEW HOLE
   AND REINSTALL SCREW

NEW SCREW LOCATION —

15°

BUICK DEALER
SERVICE
INFORMATION

Dealer Letter No.   File Under Group No.

65-116   7-4

BUICK MOTOR DIVISION   GENERAL MOTORS CORPORATION   FLINT, MICHIGAN 48550

February 19, 1965

TO ALL BUICK DEALERS

SUBJECT: New Retainer Spring For Riviera and Wildcat Chrome Wheel Medallions

The Engineering Department has released a new retainer spring which increases the retention of the center medallion on optional chrome wheels. This spring is available from the Parts Department under Group 5.859, Part No. 1373248. If early model Wildcats or Rivieras are encountered with complaints of the medallions falling off or being stolen, installation of this spring will minimize the problem.

Spring installation should be made <u>exactly</u> as shown in the illustration. If the spring is not installed in the curved portion of the tangs, it will have no effect on medallion retention.

If it should become necessary to remove the medallion, a screwdriver can be used to push the spring down and out of the rounded portion of the tangs. The spring then has no effect and the medallion can be pulled off easily.

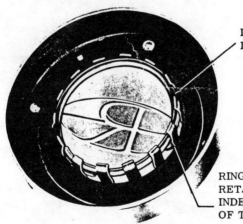

INSTALL RING
INSIDE TANGS.

RING MUST BE
RETAINED BY
INDENTED PORTION
OF TANG .

FIGURE 1

E. J. Hresko
Manager, Technical Service

WGH

CHAPTER THREE

1966 RIVIERA

BUICK DEALER
SERVICE
INFORMATION

BUICK MOTOR DIVISION • **GENERAL MOTORS CORPORATION** • **FLINT, MICHIGAN 48550**

File Under Group No.

60-12

Dealer Letter No.

66-131A

READ AND INITIAL

Dealer _____
Serv. Mgr. _____
Parts Mgr. _____
Others _____

_____ _____
_____ _____
_____ _____
_____ _____

March 25, 1966

TO ALL BUICK DEALERS

SUBJECT: 1966 Buick Engine Identification and Foreign Travel Information
  REISSUED TO REVISE PISTON AND PIN PART NUMBERS FOR 225 CU. IN. AND 300 CU. IN.
  EXPORT ENGINES AND TO CORRECT ENGINE CODE PREFIX (*).

Listed on the reverse side are the various engines used in the 1966 Buick
automobiles.

Owners contemplating travel outside the United States should be cautioned
to check on the quality of fuel available before their trip. For your
convenience, the engine chart will serve as a guide in determining engine
identification, compression ratio, fuel octane requirements, etc. Zone
Service and Parts Managers have a publication listing the octanes of the
fuels found in most countries of the world.

It should be noted that a higher octane gasoline is now available in major
Mexican cities and will eventually be available throughout the Republic.
This new fuel is known as "Pemex 100" and has a 100 octane rating (Research
Method).

If satisfactory fuels cannot be assured, the compression ratio should be
lowered by installing lower compression ratio pistons as indicated on the
chart.

NOTE: Engine damage caused by detonation as a result of the use of low
       octane fuels is not considered a defect in material or workmanship;
       therefore, cannot be considered for warranty adjustment.

/E. J. Hresko
Manager, Technical Service

Engine Mfg. Code Number Prefix	Series	Engine Description and Carburetor Equipment	Compression Ratio	Octane Requirement	Horsepower at RPM	Piston and Pin Part No.
MI	433-435-443	225 cu. in. V-6 - 2 barrel	9.0 to 1	85 Motor 93 Research	160 at 4200	1399524
MK	433-435-443	225 cu. in. V-6 - 2 barrel (export low compression)	7.6 to 1	74 Motor 83 Research	145 at 4200	1395513*
ML	434-436 444-07-17-39-67	300 cu. in. V-8 - 2 barrel	9.0 to 1	85 Motor 93 Research	210 at 4600	1399524
MM	434-436-444	300 cu. in. V-8 - 2 barrel (export low compression)	7.6 to 1	74 Motor 83 Research	195 at 4600	1395513*
MA	4439-442-44455-65 452-454	340 cu. in. V-8 - 2 barrel	9.0 to 1	85 Motor 93 Research	220 at 4000	1395184
MB	434-436-442 452-454-444	340 cu. in. V-8 - 4 barrel	10.25 to 1	90 Motor 99 Research	260 at 4000	1395312
MX	45	340 cu. in. V-8 - 2 barrel (export low compression)	8.1 to 1	76 Motor 85 Research	215 at 4000	1395513
MR	446	400 cu. in. V-8 - 4 barrel	10.25 to 1	90 Motor 99 Research	325 at 4400	1388538
MS	446	400 Cu. in. V-8 - 4 barrel	11.0 to 1	Unestablished	Unestablished	1396777
MU	446	400 cu. in. V-8 - 4 barrel	10.25 to 1	90 Motor 99 Research	340 at 4600	1388538
MT	464-466 482-484	401 cu. in. V-8 - 4 barrel	10.25 to 1	90 Motor 99 Research	325 at 4400	1388538
*MV	46-48-49	401 cu. in. V-8 - 4 barrel (export low compression)	8.75 to 1	85 Motor 93 Research	315 at 4400	1388539
MW	46-48-49	425 cu. in. V-8 - 4 barrel	10.25 to 1	90 Motor 99 Research	340 at 4400	1399211
MZ	46-49 G.S.	425 cu. in. V-8 - 2-4 barrel	10.25 to 1	90 Motor 99 Research	360 at 4400	1399211

BUICK DEALER
SERVICE
INFORMATION

BUICK
Authorized
Service

BUICK MOTOR DIVISION • GENERAL MOTORS CORPORATION • FLINT, MICHIGAN 48550

File Under Group No.	READ AND INITIAL	
64-17	Dealer	
Dealer Letter No.	Serv. Mgr.	
	Parts Mgr.	
66-128	Others	

March 11, 1966

TO ALL BUICK DEALERS

SUBJECT: 1966 Gran Sport Dual 4-Barrel and Quadrajet Carburetor Options

Carter dual 4-barrel carburetors are now available as a factory option A8 on Wildcat and Riviera Gran Sports. A Rochester Quadrajet carburetor option A9 is available on Skylark Gran Sports. These options are available only on automatic transmission equipped cars. To provide extra performance, these options include a special distributor (initial timing 12°BTC) and a high speed camshaft (same as the 1965-425 engine).

Description and Operation of Carter Dual 4-Barrel Carburetors

The 1966 Carter Model AFB dual 4-barrel carburetors are the same as the 1965 option except for choke calibration changes. These changes result in new part numbers for both front and rear carburetors. All carburetor adjustments are identical, however.

Each carburetor has a primary section (consisting of the 2-barrelled forward half) and a secondary section (consisting of the 2-barrelled rearward half). Although fuel for idling is supplied by the primary section of both carburetors, fuel for all other operations except for hard acceleration or extreme high speeds is provided by the primary section of the rear carburetor only. Only the rear carburetor is equipped with an automatic choke and a clean air system for the choke. The rear carburetor also provides connections for the positive crankcase ventilator and the distributor vacuum advance unit.

The front carburetor (primary section) has fixed idle orifices. Only the rear carburetor (primary section) has idle mixture adjusting needles and an idle speed adjustment. This speed adjustment is of the idle by-pass type; all throttle valves are closed tight, so all air flow at idle is metered by a single brass air adjustment screw in a by-pass channel.

Operation of the dual carburetor system from idle to wide open is as follows: As the accelerator pedal is gradually depressed, the primary of the rear carburetor starts to open. When it is approximately half open, the primary of the front carburetor starts to open. Next the secondary of the rear carburetor starts to open, and last, the secondary of the front carburetor starts to open. Each of the four sections opens at such a rate that all throttle valves reach the wide open position at the same time.

Throttle Linkage Adjustments - Dual 4-Barrel Carburetors

1. With choke open, move rear carburetor throttle lever to closed position, making sure that throttle valves close tightly. Move rear carburetor throttle lever to wide open position, making sure that nothing prevents lever from actually contacting wide open stop on carburetor casting. See illustration.

2. With both carburetors held at closed throttle, adjust turnbuckle until it just contacts trunnion at front carburetor, then back-off turnbuckle one turn for proper clearance and tighten lock nut.

3. With rear throttle rod held fully rearward, adjust front bolt until throttle levers of both carburetors contact their wide open stops at the same time.

Idle Speed and Mixture Adjustments - Dual 4-Barrel Carburetors

1. Remove air cleaner and gaskets.

2. Connect tachometer.

3. Start engine and run it at fast idle until upper radiator inlet is hot and choke valve is wide open.

4. On automatic transmission cars, place a safety block in front of either front wheel and apply parking brake firmly, then shift transmission into drive. Accelerate engine with left foot ready over brake pedal; if car does not move, it is safe to proceed with adjustment.

5. Make sure that all throttle valves close fully, then set idle speed at 550 RPM (with A/C off) by turning brass air adjustment screw in rear carburetor. NOTE: If idle speed cannot be adjusted fast enough, make sure engine is properly timed at 12°BTC.

6. Check positive crankcase ventilator system for proper functioning by squeezing-off ventilator hose to stop all air flow. If idle speed does not drop 60 RPM or more, PCV system must be corrected before proceeding.

7. Check idle stator switch for proper functioning by disconnecting switch connector. If idle speed does not drop, correct idle stator system before proceeding.

8. Make sure hot idle compensator valves are closed by pressing on each valve with a finger. If idle speed drops, correct idle compensator before proceeding.

9. Adjust idle mixture needles in rear carburetor to obtain highest tachometer reading. Then slowly turn needles in (leaner) one at a time until tachometer reading drops 20 RPM. Note direction of needle slot, then turn needle out (richer) exactly 1/4 turn. If tachometer reading has not returned to maximum, carefully turn needle out 1/8 turn at a time until maximum reading is just regained.

10. If idle speed is now too fast, turn idle air adjustment in to decrease speed to 550 RPM. Since this is strictly an air adjustment, this throws off the idle mixture. For this reason, always adjust idle mixture needles last.

11. Stop engine. Check dash pot adjustment by opening throttle and allowing it
     to snap closed. Time dash pot delaying action from the point where the throttle
     lever first hits the dash pot to the point where the lever stops moving. .
     Adjust dash pot as required to delay or cushion closing action two seconds.
     Tighten lock nut securely.

Rochester Quadrajet Carburetor - Skylark Gran Sport

The 1966 Rochester Model 4MC Quadrajet carburetor for use on Skylark Gran Sports
is the same as the carburetor used on 1966-425 engines except for choke calibration changes. These changes result in a new part number for the Skylark Gran
Sport carburetor. All carburetor adjustments are identical, however.

                                        E. J. Hresko
                                        Manager, Technical Service

BUICK DEALER
SERVICE
INFORMATION

BUICK MOTOR DIVISION ● **GENERAL MOTORS CORPORATION** ● **FLINT, MICHIGAN 48550**

File Under Group No.	READ AND INITIAL	
64-4	Dealer	_____
Dealer Letter No.	Serv. Mgr.	_____
	Parts Mgr.	_____
66-42	Others	_____

November 26, 1965

TO ALL BUICK DEALERS

SUBJECT: 1966 Carburetor Identification

The following list shows how to identify all 1966 carburetors using tag color, shape and code. If a part number is desired, the start of production part numbers are listed on the first page of the service manual section for each model carburetor. However, a carburetor may be modified during the model year and a new part number assigned, whereas, the tag color, shape and code will not be changed during the model year.

If a carburetor complaint of any kind is received (such as rough idle, poor mileage, poor driveability), make sure the right carburetor is installed before proceeding to other checks.

	Tag Color	Tag Shape	Tag Code
ROCHESTER 2GC CARBURETORS			
225 Eng. Man. Trans.	Silver	Triangular	YB
225 Eng. Auto. Trans.	Red	Triangular	YA
225 Eng. Auto. Trans. Cal.	Red	Square	YC
300-340 Eng. Man. Trans.	Gold	Triangular	ZB
300-340 Eng. Auto. Trans.	Blue	Triangular	ZA
300 Eng. Auto. Trans. Cal.	Blue	Square	ZC
340 Eng. Auto. Trans. Cal.	Green	Square	KC
ROCHESTER 4GC CARBURETOR			
401 Eng. Auto. Trans.	Gold	Triangular	LA
ROCHESTER 4MC CARBURETORS			
425 Eng. Auto. Trans.	Blue	Round	MA
425 Eng. Auto. Trans. Cal.	Red	1 Round-1 Square	MB
CARTER AFB CARBURETORS			
340 Eng. Man. Trans.	Silver	Triangular	SA
340 Eng. Auto. Trans.	Blue	Triangular	SB

	Tag Color	Tag Shape	Tag Code
CARTER AFB CARBURETORS			
340 Eng. Auto. Trans. Cal.	Blue	Square	SC
400 Eng. Man. Trans.	Green	Triangular	SG
400-401 Eng. Man. Trans. Cal.	Green	Square	SP
400 Eng. Auto Trans.	Black	Triangular	SJ
400 Eng. Auto. Trans. Cal.	Black	Square	SK
401 Eng. Man. Trans.	Red	Triangular	SN
401 Eng. Auto. Trans.	Gold	Triangular	SQ
401 Eng. Auto. Trans. Cal.	Gold	Square	SR

E. J. Hresko
Manager, Technical Service

SERVICE
INFORMATION

BUICK

Authorized
Service

BUICK MOTOR DIVISION   •   GENERAL MOTORS CORPORATION   •   FLINT, MICHIGAN 48550

File Under Group No.

60-11

Dealer Letter No.

66-129

READ AND INITIAL

Dealer   ————

Serv. Mgr.   ————

Parts Mgr.   ————

Others   ————

March 18, 1966

TO ALL BUICK DEALERS

SUBJECT: Taxable Horsepower Correction - 1966 Chassis Service Manual

The taxable horsepower for the Wildcat 310 300 cu. in. V-8 on
Page 60-45, Paragraph 60-2, should be 45.0 instead of 33.748.
Please note this change in the 1966 Chassis Service Manual.

The taxable horsepower for the 1966 model engines are as follows:

225 Cu. In. V-6	33.748
300 Cu. In. V-8 (Wildcat 310)	45.0
340 Cu. In. V-8 (Wildcat 350)	45.0
340 Cu. In. V-8 (Wildcat 375)	45.0
400 & 401 Cu. In. V-8 (Wildcat 445)	56.11
425 Cu. In. V-8 (Wildcat 465)	59.51

E.J. Fresko
Manager, Technical Service

BUICK

Authorized
Service

File Under Group No.

60-9

Dealer Letter No.

66-106A

READ AND INITIAL	
Dealer	_____
Serv. Mgr.	_____
Parts Mgr.	_____
Others	_____
_____	_____
_____	_____
_____	_____

BUICK MOTOR DIVISION • GENERAL MOTORS CORPORATION • FLINT, MICHIGAN 48550

March 18, 1966

TO ALL BUICK DEALERS

SUBJECT: Engine Identification - 1964 through 1966

REISSUED TO INCLUDE ENGINE WITH PREFIX "MS" TO THE 1966 USAGE.

Many inquiries have been made as to the identification of engines. Listed below are the
Engine Manufacture Code Number Prefixes for 1964 through 1966 model years. The prefixes
are intended to differentiate engine assemblies by displacement, compression ratio and
camshaft only. Refer to the appropriate service chassis manual for the proper location
of the prefix numbers.

Engine Mfg. Code Number Prefix	Engine Description	Compression Ratio
1964		
KH	225 cu. in. V-6 – 1 barrel	9.0 to 1
KJ	225 cu. in. V-6 – 1 barrel (export low compression)	7.6 to 1
KL	300 cu. in. V-8 – 2 barrel	9.0 to 1
KM	300 cu. in. V-8 – 2 barrel (export low compression)	7.6 to 1
KP	300 cu. in. V-8 – 4 barrel	11.0 to 1
KT	401 cu. in. V-8 – 4 barrel	10.25 to 1
KV	401 cu. in. V-8 – 4 barrel (export low compression)	8.75 to 1
KW	425 cu. in. V-8 – 4 barrel	10.25 to 1
KX	425 cu. in. V-8 – 2-4 barrel	10.25 to 1
1965		
LH	225 cu. in. V-6 – 1 barrel	9.0 to 1
LK	225 cu. in. V-6 – 1 barrel (export low compression)	7.6 to 1
LL	300 cu. in. V-8 – 2 barrel	9.0 to 1
LM	300 cu. in. V-8 – 2 barrel (export low compression)	7.6 to 1

Engine Mfg. Code Number Prefix	Engine Description	Compression Ratio
1965 (Cont.)		
LP	300 cu. in. V-8 - 4 barrel	10.25 to 1
LT	401 cu. in. V-8 - 4 barrel	10.25 to 1
LV	401 cu. in. V-8 - 4 barrel (export low compression)	8.75 to 1
LW	425 cu. in. V-8 - 4 barrel	10.25 to 1
LX	425 cu. in. V-8 - 2-4 barrel	10.25 to 1
1966		
MH	225 cu. in. V-6 - 2 barrel	9.0 to 1
MK	225 cu. in. V-6 - 2 barrel (export low compression)	7.6 to 1
ML	300 cu. in. V-8 - 2 barrel	9.0 to 1
MM	300 cu. in. V-8 - 2 barrel (export low compression)	7.6 to 1
MA	340 cu. in. V-8 - 2 barrel	9.0 to 1
MB	340 cu. in. V-8 - 4 barrel	10.25 to 1
MX	340 cu. in. V-8 - 2 barrel (export low compression)	8.1 to 1
MR	400 cu. in. V-8 - 4 barrel	10.25 to 1
MS	400 cu. in. V-8 - 4 barrel	11.0 to 1
MU	400 cu. in. V-8 - 4 barrel	10.25 to 1
MT	401 cu. in. V-8 - 4 barrel	10.25 to 1
MY	401 cu. in. V-8 - 4 barrel (export low compression)	8.75 to 1
MW	425 cu. in. V-8 - 4 barrel .	10.25 to 1
MZ	425 cu. in. V-8 - 2-4 barrel	10.25 to 1

E. J. Hresko
Manager, Technical Service

59

BUICK DEALER
SERVICE
INFORMATION

BUICK
Authorized
Service

BUICK MOTOR DIVISION • GENERAL MOTORS CORPORATION • FLINT, MICHIGAN 48550

File Under Group No.	READ AND INITIAL
Body - 15	Dealer _____
Dealer Letter No.	Serv. Mgr. _____
	Parts Mgr. _____
	Others _____
66-69	____ ____

January 7, 1966

TO ALL BUICK DEALERS

SUBJECT: 1966 Rivieras With Trim Combinations 651, 653, 656, or 658
Built Without Ash Trays For Rear Seat Passengers

An ash tray package, Group 12.045 Part 1361146 is now available from
the Parts Department. The package is to be used when an owner of one
of the above mentioned Rivieras requests installation. The owner should
not be charged for parts or labor. Dealer reimbursement may be obtained
by means of an AFA.

The package includes one right and one left ash tray, one right and one
left bracket, screws and a template with instructions for installation
on the door trim panel.

Flat rate allowance - .2 hrs.
Dealer Net Price is $3.00.

E. J. Wresko
Manager, Technical Service

BUICK DEALER
SERVICE
INFORMATION

BUICK MOTOR DIVISION • GENERAL MOTORS CORPORATION • FLINT, MICHIGAN 48550

File Under Group No.	READ AND INITIAL	
Body 1	Dealer	_____
Dealer Letter No.	Serv. Mgr.	_____
	Parts Mgr.	_____
66-4	Others	_____

October 8, 1965

TO ALL BUICK DEALERS

SUBJECT: Left Door Window Not Lowering Into Door On 1966 Rivieras

On some early Rivieras equipped with remote control outside rearview mirrors, the left door window will not lower the full distance into the door. It has been found that the control cables for the remote control are not fastened under the forward clip allowing the cable to catch under the window, causing the window to stop before it reaches the end of the travel. The procedure for correcting the problem is as follows:

1. Remove the two screws holding the mirror control knob plate to the trim pad. Rotate the control knob plate 360° (one full turn) counterclockwise. This rotates the cable assembly to the forward edge of the door.

    NOTE: This should position control knob plate so that when the knob is raised the mirror tilts upward.

2. With door glass down, place tool (see illustration) in front of glass and position slot of tool over cable and position cable behind the clip.

    NOTE: If cable is difficult to place behind the clip, bend clip rearward with the long prong of slotted end of the tool.

Tool may be made as shown in illustration.

E. J. Hresko
Manager, Technical Service

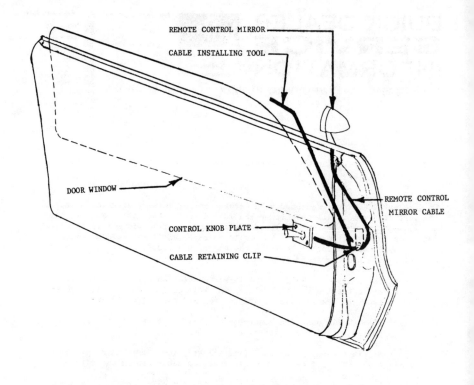

REMOTE CONTROL MIRROR

CABLE INSTALLING TOOL

DOOR WINDOW

REMOTE CONTROL
MIRROR CABLE

CONTROL KNOB PLATE

CABLE RETAINING CLIP

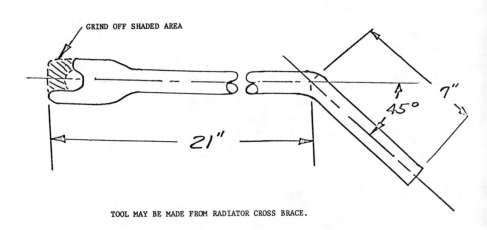

GRIND OFF SHADED AREA

21"

7"

45°

TOOL MAY BE MADE FROM RADIATOR CROSS BRACE.

BUICK DEALER
SERVICE
INFORMATION

BUICK MOTOR DIVISION • GENERAL MOTORS CORPORATION • FLINT, MICHIGAN 48550

BUICK
Authorized
Service

File Under Group No.

Body - 18

Dealer Letter No.

66-100

February 11, 1966

TO ALL BUICK DEALERS

SUBJECT: Changes in Color Standard - Gold Metallic, Paint Code G -
1966 49000 Series

The above color standard was revised slighty for production and
appearance purposes. This resulted in a very slight change in
the formulation. Accordingly, a first and second type refinish
color is required in service.

Body Number EUC 82460 represents the first car painted with the
new material.

The chart below designates the refinish colors for early production
and for late production.

Source	Early Production	Late Production
Rinshed-Mason	A-1809	A-1809 No. 2
Ditzler	DDL-22661 Batch V-4392 & Batch V-6097	DDL-22661 Colors with a Higher Batch Number
DuPont	Not Released	4715-L

E. J. Hresko
Manager, Technical Service

BUICK DEALER
SERVICE
INFORMATION

BUICK
Authorized
Service

File Under Group No.

Body - 36

Dealer Letter No.

66-170

READ AND INITIAL

Dealer _____
Serv. Mgr. _____
Parts Mgr. _____
Others _____

_____ _____
_____ _____
_____ _____

BUICK MOTOR DIVISION • GENERAL MOTORS CORPORATION • FLINT, MICHIGAN 48550

July 8, 1966

TO ALL BUICK DEALERS

SUBJECT: Addition of Front Door Hinge Torque Rods - 1966 Rivieras

A new front door hinge torque rod is now being used on 1966 Rivieras which reduces door opening effort without materially affecting closing effort.

The torque rod is available for service on complaint cars. Installation is described and illustrated in the following procedure.

1. Procure two torque rods (Gr. 10.454 - Part No. 7684992) and two torque rod retainers (Gr. 10.454 - Part No. 7693141) and two bolts (Gr. 10.463 - Part No. 4405449). The rod and retainer are common parts for both right and left sides.

   NOTE: Part No. 4405449 is the bolt used on all Riviera body hinge attachments, door side.

2. As shown in the illustration, the torque rod is secured under the upper hinge lower rearward bolt, body side, on right doors (See View "A") and under the lower hinge upper rearward bolt on left doors (See View "B"). The existing hinge bolt cannot be used because the rod thickness prevents full thread engagement. Use new bolt (Part No. 4405449) for each rod attachment.

3. With door fully opened, install torque rod(s) and retainer(s) as depicted in the illustration, curved end first. The "curved end" slides behind hinge straps.

Flat Rate Time to install one new torque rod is .2 hr.; both, .4 hr.

E. J. Hresko
Manager, Technical Service

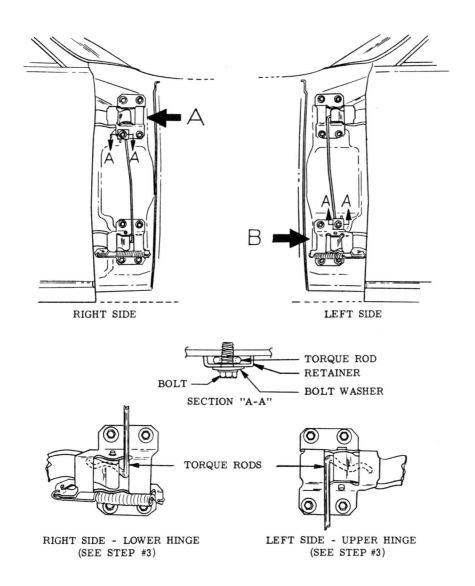

RIGHT SIDE

LEFT SIDE

SECTION "A-A"

TORQUE ROD
RETAINER
BOLT
BOLT WASHER

TORQUE RODS

RIGHT SIDE - LOWER HINGE
(SEE STEP #3)

LEFT SIDE - UPPER HINGE
(SEE STEP #3)

BUICK DEALER
SERVICE
INFORMATION

BUICK
Authorized
Service

File Under Group No.

64-12

Dealer Letter No.

66-104

READ AND INITIAL

Dealer _____
Serv. Mgr. _____
Parts Mgr. _____
Others _____
_____ _____
_____ _____
_____ _____
_____ _____

BUICK MOTOR DIVISION • GENERAL MOTORS CORPORATION • FLINT, MICHIGAN 48550

February 25, 1966

TO ALL BUICK DEALERS

SUBJECT: Engine Timing and Idle Adjustments - 1964 through 1966

1964-5-6 Specifications

Timing	Idle
5° B.T.C. (V-6 Engine)	550 RPM in Drive
2-1/2° B.T.C. (300-340 Engines)	550 RPM in Drive
2-1/2° B.T.C. (400-401-425 Engines)	500 RPM in Drive
12° B.T.C. (Dual 4-B Auto Trans. or Skylark Gran Sport Quadrajet)	500 RPM in Drive

NOTE: If car is equipped with California air injection reactor and/or air (with conditioner off), add 50 RPM to idle specifications.

Timing Adjustment

1. Adjust contact point dwell angle to 30 degrees.

2. Adjust idle speed to specifications above.

3. Disconnect distributor vacuum hose.

4. Adjust timing to specifications above.

5. Reconnect distributor vacuum hose.

Idle Adjustment

1. With engine warm, place automatic transmission car in drive.

2. Adjust idle speed to specifications above.

3. Make certain idle stator switch is closed by disconnecting switch connector. If idle speed does not decrease, switch is not closed; adjust idle stator switch, then readjust idle speed to specifications.

4. Connect a vacuum gage, if available, to intake manifold vacuum.

5. Adjust idle mixture needles, one at a time. Turn needle to obtain highest tachometer or vacuum gage reading. Then slowly turn needle in (leaner) until tachometer reading drops 20 RPM or until vacuum gage reading drops 1/2 inch. Note direction of needle slot, then turn needle out (richer) exactly 1/4 turn and observe tachometer or vacuum gage. If reading has not returned to maximum, carefully turn needle out 1/8 turn at a time until maximum reading is just regained.

6. If either needle setting is changed much, always recheck other needle setting since they affect each other.

7. If idle speed is now too fast, reduce speed to specifications and recheck mixture adjustment.

For your information, the improved idle mixture adjustment described in Step 5 is also the best adjustment procedure for past model cars. It will give the best and most economical performance at idle and at lower speeds for all cars; however, it is especially important that A.I.R. equipped cars be adjusted to the "lean side of best idle" using this procedure to keep hydrocarbon and carbon monoxide emissions to a minimum.

E. J. Hresko
Manager, Technical Service

File Under Group No.
64-3

Dealer Letter No.

66-25

READ AND INITIAL

Dealer _____
Serv. Mgr. _____
Parts Mgr. _____
Others _____

_____ _____
_____ _____
_____ _____

October 29, 1965

TO ALL BUICK DEALERS

SUBJECT: Sticking Electro-Cruise Engagement Switches - 1966 Rivieras

A few cases were reported in the factory of sticking engagement switches on Electro-Cruise equipped Rivieras. The sticking can occur internally in the speedometer head or at the point where the engagement shaft goes through the plastic lens. We are recommending that you check all Rivieras in stock, and all other Rivieras as they come in for service, for sticking switches.

Check for a sticking engagement switch as follows:

1. Set Electro-Cruise dial at 30 and 90. With dial in both positions, depressed engagement switch must return to center detent position without help.

2. If switch sticks or drags, check speedo cable for improper routing, kinks, binds, etc. and correct. Also check A/C ducts or wire harnesses for hitting or pulling on speedo cluster, causing deflection in the speedo head which may be binding the Electro-Cruise switch shaft against the plastic lens.

3. After making all corrections in step 2, if switch still sticks, remove instrument cluster. Remove lens and enlarge 1/4 inch shaft hole to 5/16 inch. After enlarging lens hole, put a _thin_ film of 4X silicone grease on switch shaft where cruise wire crosses shaft.

4. Position speedo head in cluster to give best centering of shaft in hole through lens.

5. Reinstall instrument cluster, being careful to get best possible speedo cable route.

E. J. Hresko
Manager, Technical Service

BUICK DEALER
SERVICE
INFORMATION

BUICK Authorized Service

File Under Group No.

Body - 27

Dealer Letter No.

66-130

READ AND INITIAL

Dealer _____
Serv. Mgr. _____
Parts Mgr. _____
Others _____

_____
_____
_____
_____

BUICK MOTOR DIVISION   •   GENERAL MOTORS CORPORATION   •   FLINT, MICHIGAN 48550

March 18, 1966

TO ALL BUICK DEALERS

SUBJECT: Fabric Roof Cover - 1966 49000 Series

A fabric roof cover option has been added for the 1966 Riviera. The option includes a vinyl fabric roof cover, a new rear compartment front grille and three new moldings.

Service procedures are described and illustrated as follows:

FABRIC ROOF COVER

The procedures covering the description, removal and installation of the vinyl roof cover are as described in the 1966 Body Service Manual, Section 5.

REAR COMPARTMENT FRONT PANEL GRILLE

The textured surface of the rear compartment front panel grille requires a special paint, although application remains conventional.

REAR COMPARTMENT FRONT PANEL GRILLE PAINT

SOURCE	COLOR	
	White	Black
Ditzler	DDL 8659	DDL 9339
DuPont	9332-L and No. 4528 Flatting Compound NOTE: Use mixture of 1 pint 9332-L and 1 ounce No. 4528 Flatting Compound.	9333-L and No. 4528 Flatting Compound NOTE: Use mixture of 1 pint 9333-L and 2 ounces No. 4528 Flatting Compound.
Rinshed-Mason	1 U9992 and No. 849 Suede Concentrate NOTE: Use mixture of 2 parts 1 U9992 and 1 part No. 849 Suede Concentrate.	A-946 and No. 849 Suede Concentrate NOTE: Use mixture of 2 parts A-946 and 1 part No. 849 Suede Concentrate.

EXTERIOR MOLDINGS

The new moldings can be removed in the following manner:

1. The roof panel front cover finishing molding, Item 1, is attached by one screw at the windshield end of the molding. To gain access to the screw and remove the molding the windshield reveal upper molding. Item 2, and the windshield pillar drip molding, Item 3, must be removed.

2. The quarter belt reveal molding assembly, Item 4, is attached to the quarter panel by means of (4) snap-on clips and a bolt and clip assembly. The nut is located adjacent to the compartment front panel grille and is accessible from inside the rear compartment.

3. The compartment front panel grille molding, Item 5, is attached to the compartment front panel by means of (7) clip and bolt assemblies. To gain access to the nuts the compartment front panel grille must be removed.

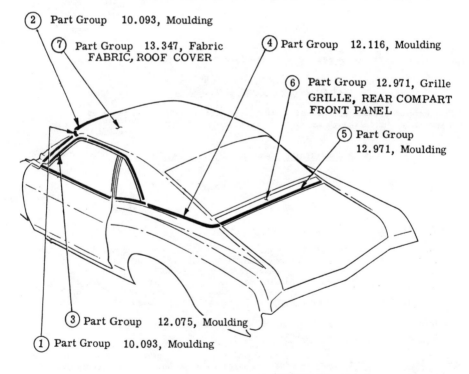

② Part Group   10.093, Moulding

⑦ Part Group   13.347, Fabric
  FABRIC, ROOF COVER

④ Part Group   12.116, Moulding

⑥ Part Group   12.971, Grille
  GRILLE, REAR COMPART
  FRONT PANEL

⑤ Part Group
  12.971, Moulding

③ Part Group   12.075, Moulding

① Part Group   10.093, Moulding

E. J. Hresko
Manager, Technical Service

BUICK DEALER
SERVICE
INFORMATION

BUICK

Authorized
Service

File Under Group No.

120-5

Dealer Letter No.

66-54

READ AND INITIAL

Dealer _____
Serv. Mgr. _____
Parts Mgr. _____
Others _____
_____
_____
_____
_____

BUICK MOTOR DIVISION • GENERAL MOTORS CORPORATION • FLINT, MICHIGAN 48550

December 10, 1965

TO ALL BUICK DEALERS

SUBJECT: Poorly Grounded Riviera Headlamp Motor Control Relays

A few cases have been encountered where relays would not operate because they were not securely fastened down and therefore not properly grounded. These relays were replaced needlessly, since they later checked-out okay. A poorly grounded relay could result in inoperative headlamps which operate intermittently.

For this reason, whenever a relay is found which does not operate properly, first make sure all wires are connected correctly, then check the mounting screws to make sure they are tightened securely. Replace any screw which will not tighten with the next larger size rust-proof screw; make sure the oversize screw is tightened securely.

E. J. Hresko
Manager, Technical Service

CHAPTER FOUR

1967 RIVIERA

BUICK DEALER
SERVICE INFORMATION
BULLETIN

BUICK MOTOR DIVISION • GENERAL MOTORS CORPORATION • FLINT, MICHIGAN 48550

September 30, 1966

TO ALL BUICK DEALERS

SUBJECT: 1967 Buick Engine Identification and Foreign Travel
Information

Listed on the reverse side are the various engines used in the 1967
Buick automobiles.

Owners contemplating travel outside the United States should be
cautioned to check on the quality of fuel available before their
trip. For your convenience, the engine chart will serve as a
guide in determining engine identification, compression ratio,
fuel octane requirements, etc. Zone Service and Parts Managers
have a publication listing the octanes of the fuels found in most
countries of the world.

It should be noted that a higher octane gasoline is now available
in major Mexian cities and will eventually be available throughout the Republic. This new fuel is known as "Pemex 100" and has
a 100 octane rating (Research Method).

If satisfactory fuels cannot be assured, the compression ratio
should be lowered by installing lower compression ratio pistons
as indicated on the chart.

NOTE: Engine damage caused by detonation as a result of the use
of low octane fuels is not considered a defect in material
or workmanship; therefore, cannot be considered for warranty
adjustment.

Service Department
BUICK MOTOR DIVISION

Engine Mfg. Code Number Prefix	Series	Engine Description and Carburetor Equipment	Compression Ratio	Octane Requirement	Horsepower at RPM	Piston and Pin Part No.
NH	433-435-433	225 cu. in. V-6 - 2 barrel	9.0 to 1	85 Motor 93 Research	160 at 4200	1399524
NK	433-435-443	225 cu. in. V-6 - 2 barrel (export low compression)	7.6 to 1	74 Motor 83 Research	145 at 4200	1395513
NL	434-436 444-07-17-67	300 cu. in. V-8 - 2 barrel	9.0 to 1	85 Motor 93 Research	210 at 4400	1399524
NM	434-436-444	300 cu. in. V-8 - 2 barrel (export low compression)	7.6 to 1	74 Motor 83 Research	195 at 4400	1395513
NA	4439-442- 44455-65 452-454	340 cu. in. V-8 - 2 barrel	9.0 to 1	85 Motor 93 Research	220 at 4200	1395184
NB	434-436-442 452-454-444	340 cu. in. V-8 - 4 barrel	10.25 to 1	90 Motor 99 Research	260 at 4200	1395312
NX	452-454	340 cu. in. V-8 - 2 barrel (export low compression	8.1 to 1	76 Motor 85 Research	215 at 4200	1395513
NR	446	400 cu. in. V-8 - 4 barrel	10.25 to 1	90 Motor 99 Research	340 at 5000	1395592
ND or MD	464-466-482 484-494	430 cu. in. V-8 - 4 barrel	10.25 to 1	90 Motor 99 Research	360 at 5000	1395521
NE	464-466-482 484-494	430 cu. in. V-8 - 4 barrel (export low compression)	8.75 to 1	85 Motor 93 Research	330 at 5000	1395653

BUICK DEALER
SERVICE TECHNICAL
BULLETIN

BUICK MOTOR DIVISION • **GENERAL MOTORS CORPORATION** • **FLINT, MICHIGAN 48550**

October 14, 1966

TO ALL BUICK DEALERS

SUBJECT: Exhaust Valve Stem Seals - 1967 400 and 430 Cubic Inch Engines

Beginning with engine code number ND 087 or NR 087, revised cylinder heads for the 1967 400 and 430 cubic inch engines, which incorportate exhaust valve stem seals in addition to the existing intake valve stem seals, have gone into production.

The incorporation of exhaust valve seals will give greater uniformity in overhead oil control in these two new engines for 1967.

If replacement of these new seals is required, use valve stem seals (Group 0.308, Part No. 1396858) that are now used on the intake valves.

Service Department
BUICK MOTOR DIVISION

BUICK DEALER
SERVICE INFORMATION
BULLETIN

BUICK MOTOR DIVISION • GENERAL MOTORS CORPORATION • FLINT, MICHIGAN 48550

October 28, 1966

TO ALL BUICK DEALERS

SUBJECT: Hydraulic Valve Lifter Identification - 1967 Engines

A new hydraulic valve lifter is being used for the 1967 400 and 430 cubic inch engine. It has a slight spherical shaped base which, when used with the new 400 and 430 camshaft, having tapered lobes, produces camshaft thrust rearward and induces lifter rotation. If this new lifter is used in the 225, 300, or 340 cubic inch engine, camshaft stress on the valve lifter will cause a spalling effect. Therefore, it is important that correct valve lifters be used in each engine. Refer to the illustrations for valve lifter identification.

The service valve lifter for the 225, 300, and 340 cubic inch engine, (Group No. 0.459, Part No. 5232245), can be identified by the three grooves in the body; however, the production valve lifters have the bottom groove omitted.

The service valve lifter for the 400 and 430 cubic inch engine, (Group No. 0.459, Part No. 5231740), can be identified by the ink stamp HL15 on the body and the body is free from grooves.

Note: Since lifters previously used on past models had external groove in them for identification, the 1967 lifter for the 400 and 430 cubic inch engine can easily be identified by the plain body lifter having no external grooves.

The production 400 and 430 valve lifter has copper flashing on the push rod seat for assembly identification purposes, but it may wear off during service. Since the spherical shape base is so slight, it should be disregarded for identification purposes.

Service Department
BUICK MOTOR DIVISION

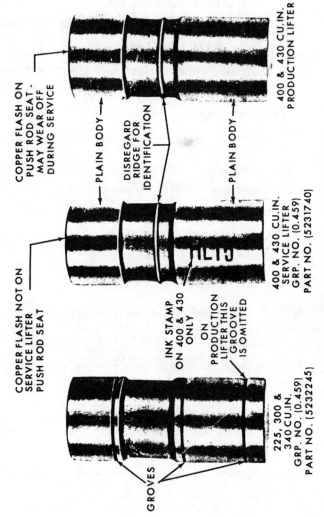

COPPER FLASH ON PUSH ROD SEAT - MAY WEAR OFF DURING SERVICE

COPPER FLASH NOT ON SERVICE LIFTER PUSH ROD SEAT

PLAIN BODY

DISREGARD RIDGE FOR IDENTIFICATION

PLAIN BODY

INK STAMP ON 400 & 430 ONLY

ON PRODUCTION LIFTER THIS GROOVE IS OMITTED

GROVES

400 & 430 CU.IN. PRODUCTION LIFTER

400 & 430 CU.IN. SERVICE LIFTER GRP. NO. (0.459) PART NO. (5231740)

225, 300 & 340 CU.IN. GRP. NO. (0.459) PART NO. (5232245)

1967 HYDRAULIC VALVE LIFTER IDENTIFICATION

78

INFORMATION BULLETIN NUMBER		DEALER FILE	
		Model Year	1967
67-I-18		File in Group	60
		Number	4

BUICK DEALER
SERVICE INFORMATION
BULLETIN

BUICK MOTOR DIVISION • GENERAL MOTORS CORPORATION • FLINT, MICHIGAN 48550

November 4, 1966

TO ALL BUICK DEALERS

SUBJECT: 1967 Engine Oil Dipstick Information - All Series

A. As in the past, an engine oil dipstick usage chart is published for new model cars to ensure that correct dipsticks are used so that oil level is correct after crankcase refill and also, so that consumption complaints are not the result of incorrect dipsticks.

Listed below are dipstick part numbers which are stamped on the stick shaft and the engine in which they should be used:

Year	Group No.	Part No.	Engine Usage
1967	1.516	1379886 or 1368547	All V-6 Power Brake
1965-67	1.516	1374247	All V-6 Less Power Brake
1966-67	1.516	1368546	300 Eng. Less A.I.R.
1966-67	1.516	1377739	300 Eng. A.I.R. (Calif. Cars)
1966-67	1.516	1377740	340 Eng. A.I.R. (Calif. Cars)
1966-67	1.516	1375251	340 Eng. Less A.I.R.
1967	1.516	1379886	400 Eng.
1967	1.516	1373406	430 Eng.

B.. Some early production 400 cu. in. engines may be found in which a 430 cu. in. engine dipstick has been used. Also, some 225 and 400 cu. in. engines may be found with the correct part number (1379886) stamped on the dipstick blade, but the oil level markings are incorrect. Both of these conditions would result in incorrect oil reading on the dipstick.

For correct usage of dipstick for the 225 and the 400 cu. in. engine refer to the illustration.

C. With the new designed 430 cu. in. engine, the clearance be-
    tween dipstick and crankshaft is closer than the other engines
    available for 1967. Therefore, it is very important that the
    430 cu. in. dipstick be free of any bends to avoid striking
    the crankshaft. Also if the dipstick is bent on any engine,
    improper oil reading could result.

                            Service Department
                            BUICK MOTOR DIVISION

CORRECT 430 CU. IN. DIP STICK

ADD 1 QT. OPERATING RANGE CAP. 4 QTS. 1373406 M

11/16"

INCORRECT 225 AND 400 CU. IN. DIP STICK

ADD 1 QT. OPERATING-RANGE CAP 4 QTS 1379886

5/8"

CORRECT *225 AND 400 CU. IN. DIP STICK

ADD 1 QT OPERATING RANGE CAP 4 QTS 1379886

1"

*NOTE: EARLY PRODUCTION
225 CU. IN. ENGINE USING
PART NO 1368547 IS CORRECT
MARKINGS ARE IDENTICAL
TO PART NO. 1379886

BUICK DEALER
SERVICE INFORMATION
BULLETIN

BUICK MOTOR DIVISION • **GENERAL MOTORS CORPORATION** • **FLINT, MICHIGAN 48550**

October 28, 1966

TO ALL BUICK DEALERS

SUBJECT: Spark Plug Wire Routing - All 1967 V-8 Engines

Cross-firing can occur if ignition wires lie parallel
and close together for several inches. Since cylinders No. 5 and 7 are adjacent and the firing order
is 1-8-4-3-6-5-7-2, we have the cross-fire possibility.
Therefore, whenever spark plug wires are removed for
any reason, it is very important that they be rein-
stalled as described below and as shown in the illustration on back of page.

Wire No. 7 must be routed in the top notches and wire
No. 5 must be routed in the bottom notches of the clips.
Wires No. 1 and 3 are routed in the two middle notches,
with No. 3 above No. 1.

Service Department
BUICK MOTOR DIVISION

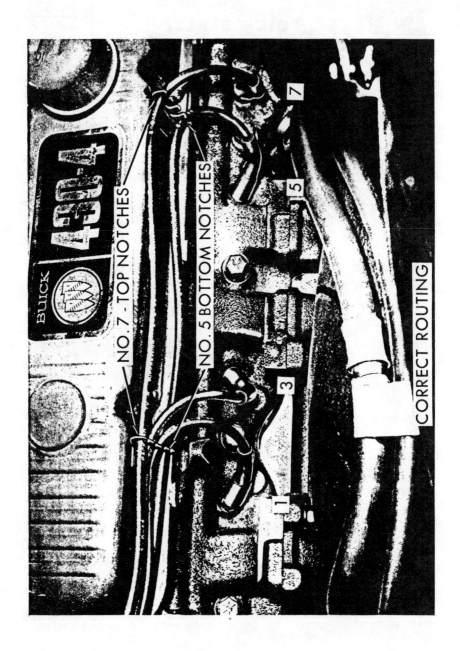

BUICK 455-4

NO. 7 - TOP NOTCHES

NO. 5 BOTTOM NOTCHES

7

5

3

1

CORRECT ROUTING

INFORMATION
BULLETIN
NUMBER

67-I-35

BUICK DEALER
SERVICE INFORMATION
BULLETIN

DEALER FILE	
Model Year	1967
File in Group	60
Number	6

BUICK MOTOR DIVISION • GENERAL MOTORS CORPORATION • FLINT, MICHIGAN 48550

January 6, 1967

TO ALL BUICK DEALERS

SUBJECT: Valve Rocker Arm Shaft Attachment Bolt Torque - 1967
400 and 430 cu. in. Engines

A few early production engines were released where the rocker arm
shaft to cylinder head attachment bolts (280M, 5/16-18, 1.62" in
length) were used in place of the present 300M bolt (5/16-18, 1.8"
in length). The correct torque for the 280M bolt is 18 lb. ft.,
and 25-35 lb. ft. for the 300M bolt.

If replacement of this bolt (280M) is required, the 280M bolt must
be used, as the cylinder head bolt hole is not drilled deep enough
to use the presently released 300M bolt (group No. 0.349 Part No.
1381272).

Refer to illustration for 280M and 300M bolt identification.

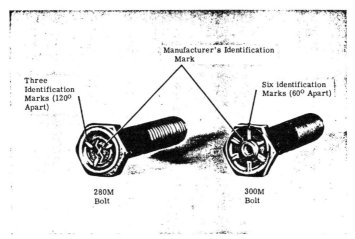

Manufacturer's Identification
Mark

Three
Identification
Marks (120°
Apart)

Six identification
Marks (60° Apart)

280M
Bolt

300M
Bolt

Service Department
BUICK MOTOR DIVISION

BUICK DEALER
SERVICE TECHNICAL
BULLETIN

BUICK MOTOR DIVISION • GENERAL MOTORS CORPORATION • FLINT, MICHIGAN 48550

September 23, 1966

TO ALL BUICK DEALERS

SUBJECT: Idle Stator Switch Adjustment - All 1967 Super Turbine
300 and 400 Transmissions

There is a possibility that a few early production 1967 Super Turbine
300 and 400 transmission equipped cars were built with misadjusted
idle stator switches. A misadjusted idle stator switch will cause
two problems: (1) transmission stator will remain in high angle
at all times, (2) transmission stator will remain in low angle at
idle but will operate properly during other phases of operation.

If the idle stator switch is misadjusted so the stator will remain
in high angle at all times, the transmission will feel sluggish or
give the impression of slipping on acceleration. This condition will
become more noticeable as the weather becomes colder.

If the idle stator switch is misadjusted so the stator will remain
in low angle at idle the car will have an excessive amount of "creep"
in any driving range at idle. Also this condition may aggravate
roughness at idle.

Note: Under no circumstances should a transmission be removed from
a car to attempt a correction on the above complaints until
the transmission has been proven to be malfunctioning.

In order to prevent a customer complaint arising from a misadjusted
switch, we recommend that you direct special attention to checking
for misadjusted idle stator switches on all 1967 automatic transmission equipped cars according to the 1967 New Car Pre-Delivery
Inspection and Adjustment Check Sheet. See Item #6. "Road Test" and
Item #3. of the 1967 Buick New Car Pre-Delivery Specification Sheet.

Service Department
BUICK MOTOR DIVISION

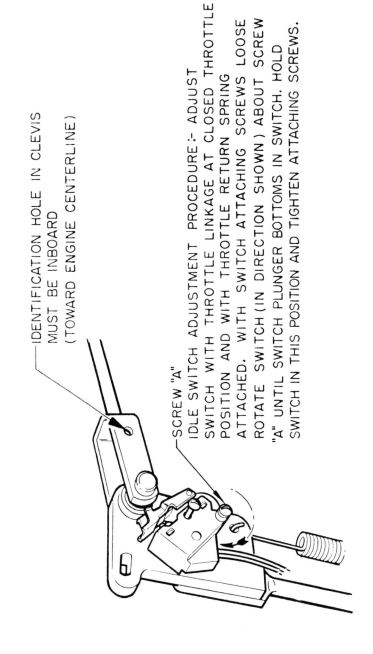

IDENTIFICATION HOLE IN CLEVIS
MUST BE INBOARD
(TOWARD ENGINE CENTERLINE)

SCREW "A"
IDLE SWITCH ADJUSTMENT PROCEDURE :- ADJUST
SWITCH WITH THROTTLE LINKAGE AT CLOSED THROTTLE
POSITION AND WITH THROTTLE RETURN SPRING
ATTACHED. WITH SWITCH ATTACHING SCREWS LOOSE
ROTATE SWITCH (IN DIRECTION SHOWN) ABOUT SCREW
"A" UNTIL SWITCH PLUNGER BOTTOMS IN SWITCH. HOLD
SWITCH IN THIS POSITION AND TIGHTEN ATTACHING SCREWS.

BUICK DEALER
SERVICE TECHNICAL
BULLETIN

BUICK MOTOR DIVISION • GENERAL MOTORS CORPORATION • FLINT, MICHIGAN 48550

November 4, 1966

TO ALL BUICK DEALERS

SUBJECT: Pump Rod Location Change - 1967 Quadrajet Carburetors Used
With 400 Auto. Transmission, 400 A.I.R. Auto. Transmission
and 430 A.I.R. Engines

Early 1967 Quadrajet Carburetors, on the three engines mentioned
above, have the pump rod installed in the inner hole of the pump
lever. When operating during extreme hot weather or at high al-
titude, this causes too large a pump shot, resulting in "pump
slug". All later production carburetors on these engines have
the pump rod located in the outer hole to reduce the pump shot.

If a hesitation or stumble complaint is encountered which is
worse when the engine is hot, make sure the pump rod is in the
outer hole on any of these three engines. If not, move the pump
rod to the outer hole. Caution: The pump rod must be bent
slightly to prevent the rod from interfering with the throttle
lever, when it is positioned in the outer hole.

Proceed as follows:

1. Remove upper end of pump rod from inner hole.

2. With throttle closed, position pump lever so that outer hole
    aligns with end of pump rod; now force rod outward past outer
    hole to a point flush with end of pump lever.

3. Place rod in outer hole and check for 1/32 inch clearance
    with throttle lever.

4. If clearance is satisfactory, reinstall hair pin clip.

If the pump height is adjusted correctly with the pump rod in
the inner hole, no adjustment is needed when changing the rod
to the outer hole. Correct adjustment is 9/32 inch in inner hole,
or 13/32 inch in outer hole. With pump height adjusted to 9/32
inch in inner hole, moving pump rod to outer hole automatically
makes pump height 13/32 inch.

See Figure 64-34 in the 1967 Chassis Service Manual for
the adjustment procedure.

NOTE: If complaints of hesitation or flatness are received
during cold weather, it may be necessary to move the
pump rod back to the inner hole for cold weather
operation only.

Service Department
BUICK MOTOR DIVISION

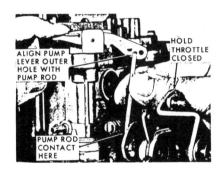

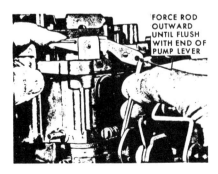

BUICK DEALER
SERVICE INFORMATION
BULLETIN

BUICK MOTOR DIVISION • GENERAL MOTORS CORPORATION • FLINT, MICHIGAN 48550

April 28, 1967

TO ALL BUICK DEALERS

SUBJECT: Replacement of Power Steering (Return Hose-to-Pump) Clamp-ALL SERIES

A change is being made in the assembly plants to replace the screw-type power steering return hose-to-pump clamp with a pinch-type clamp. This change applies to all 1967 after jobs with power steering.

USE

If the pinch-type clamp is removed, it cannot be re-used and must be discarded. The screw-type clamp (Part Number 274337) is being retained for service replacements on all 1967-68 cars with power steering. Because of the special tool required for installation of the pinch-type clamp, the screw-type clamp will remain released in power steering packages 981207-981208-981209.

REMOVAL AND INSTALLATION

In removing the pinch-type clamp, use side cutters to cut the clamp being careful not to damage the hose or loosen the pump inlet. At hose re-installation, the screw-type clamp (Part Number 274337) is to be installed and tightened to provide a leak-proof connection.

Service Department
BUICK MOTOR DIVISION

INFORMATION BULLETIN NUMBER		DEALER FILE	
		Model Year	1967
67-I-6	**BUICK DEALER** **SERVICE INFORMATION** **BULLETIN**	File in Group	120
		Number	1

BUICK MOTOR DIVISION • **GENERAL MOTORS CORPORATION** • **FLINT, MICHIGAN 48550**

September 30, 1966

TO ALL BUICK DEALERS

SUBJECT: New Electrical Features in All 1967 Buicks

Fusible Links

All series Buicks have fusible links located between the starting motor post and the lower ends of the main supply wires. These links are the weakest point in the electrical supply system for the complete car, and, as such, will act like a fuse for every wiring harness in the car. Every electrical accessory is still protected by a fuse or circuit breaker, of course, but fusible links have been added to protect the wiring harnesses before the fuses. In the past, if a wire became grounded in the portion between the battery and the fuse block, a long section of the wire would burn out, making replacement of a complete wiring harness necessary. These wiring harnesses were generally expensive, complicated and hard to get at; they often required many hours of a skilled electrician's time to replace them. Now, with the fusible links, a short or ground in any unfused wire will only cause a six inch link at the starting motor to burn out. Because of its location, possibility of a fire, such as was sometimes caused by a burned-out wiring harness, is very remote.

All series except Rivieras have two fusible links connected to the starting motor post:

1. In the No. 12 red wire circuit which, for safety purposes, supplies only the headlight circuit.

2. In the No. 10 red wire circuit which supplies all electrical units except the headlights. Rivieras, to make the ammeter read correctly, have only a No. 10 red wire to supply all electrical units including the headlights; Rivieras, therefore, have only one fusible link.

A fusible link is simply a short section of wire which is several sizes smaller gauge than the wire in the circuit which it protects. The No. 10 wire supply circuit is protected by a No. 14 brown link; the No. 12 wire headlight circuit is protected by a No. 16 black link. If a short or ground occurs in either of these circuits, the fusible link will melt before the insulation is damaged elsewhere in the circuit.

A burned-out fusible link would be indicated by:

1. All electrical accessories dead except headlights; or, headlights dead but all other electrical units working, on all series except Rivieras.

2. All electrical units dead on Rivieras.

3. Starter dead - won't even click. Even with a nearly dead battery, the
   starter solenoid will generally engage; therefore, no click means no
   solenoid action, possibly due to a burned-out fusible link.

4. For a positive test for a burned-out fusible link turn blower switch to
   a high speed position. Connect a test light or a voltmeter between
   positive battery post and No. 10 red wire screw terminal at cowl. If
   test light lights brightly or if voltmeter reads battery voltage, fusible
   link is burned out.

For the procedure recommended for replacing a burned-out fusible link, see
page 120-7 in the 1967 Buick Chassis Service Manual.

Brake Failure Warning Light

The brake failure warning light circuit uses the same light as the parking
brake warning light circuit -- a red "BRAKE" signal light in the instrument
cluster. When this signal lights during service brake application, this is
a warning that either the front or the rear half of the dual brake system
has lost hydraulic pressure and is failing to provide effective braking.

The switch to operate the brake failure warning light is in a simple spring-
centered balance valve subjected to front brake line pressure on one side
and rear brake line pressure on the other side. A difference of 150 PSI between these pressures, as will occur if one system fails, causes the valve
to move from center and to contact an electrode which grounds the brake
warning light. In addition, the driver will notice increased brake pedal
travel and decreased brake effectiveness.

The recommended procedure for checking operation of the brake failure warning
light switch is shown on page 120-16 of the 1967 Buick Chassis Service Manual.

Hazard Warning Flasher

The hazard warning feature (standard on all cars) is a system which when
turned on, causes all four turn signal lamps to flash simultaneously. This
system makes use of the regular turn signal wiring and light bulbs, but has
a separate supply wire, flasher unit and off-on switch. This makes it possible, when leaving a car with the hazard flasher operating, to lock the
ignition switch and car doors.

The hazard warning flasher is turned on by pushing in on the "FLASHER"
button located just below the steering wheel on the right side of the steering
column. The hazard flasher system should always be turned off, by pulling
the button out, before the car is driven. However, the system is selfcan-
celling whenever the steering wheel is rotated 3/8 turn or more.

Service Department
BUICK MOTOR DIVISION

INFORMATION BULLETIN NUMBER		DEALER FILE	
		Model Year	1967
67-I-77		File in Group	50
		Number	5

BUICK DEALER
SERVICE INFORMATION
BULLETIN

BUICK MOTOR DIVISION • GENERAL MOTORS CORPORATION • FLINT, MICHIGAN 48550

April 28, 1967

TO ALL BUICK DEALERS

SUBJECT: Disc Brake Metering Valve Change - 1967 Models Equipped With Disc Brake Option

Beginning on January 6, 1967 on Flint built cars equipped with the Disc Brake option, a new metering valve (4.690-1383400) is being used.

The new metering valve will be used in production at the various assembly plants as supplies of the first type metering valve (4.690-1382483) are exhausted.

The external appearance of the new metering valve is the same as the metering valve used since the beginning of 1967 production. The new metering valve can, however, be identified by a "tulip" on the outer end of the push rod. See Figures 1 & 2.

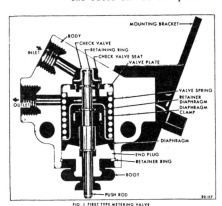

FIG. 1 FIRST TYPE METERING VALVE

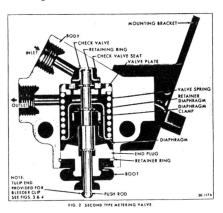

FIG. 2 SECOND TYPE METERING VALVE

Changes in the size of the bleed holes of the valve plate reduce the possibility of having a noisy metering valve. This noise can best be described as a "click" that is heard during rapid application of brakes. The "click" sound appears to come from the area behind the instrument panel.

Front disc brakes with second type metering valve, can be bled in the same manner as with first type valve, however, due to the reduction in size of internal bleeder holes, it is recommended that a Metering Valve Bleeder Clip be used when bleeding is required. See Figures 3 & 4.

The Bleeder Clip is available from the following two sources:

KENT-MOORE CORP.
28635 Mound Road
Warren, Michigan 48092
Tool # J-22742
Price $1.90

BORROUGHS TOOL & EQUIPMENT CORP.
2429 North Burdick Street
Kalamazoo, Michigan 49007
Tool # BT-6751
Price $1.90

FIG. 3
KENT-MOORE CLIP

FIG. 4
BORROUGHS CLIP

Metering Valve 4.690-1382483 will continue to be used for Service Replacement on 1967 43-44000 Series only. Metering Valve 4.690-1383400 should be used for Service Replacement on all 45-46-49000 Series.

Service Department
BUICK MOTOR DIVISION

BUICK DEALER
SERVICE INFORMATION
BULLETIN

BUICK MOTOR DIVISION • GENERAL MOTORS CORPORATION • FLINT, MICHIGAN 48550

September 23, 1966

TO ALL BUICK DEALERS

SUBJECT: Front Brake Wheel Cylinder Size - 1967 49000 Series

As noted in the 1967 Buick Service Manual, some early 1967 Rivieras
are equipped with 1-1/8" front wheel cylinders (first type). Beginning with serial number 494877H901346, 1-3/16" front wheel cylinders
(second type) are being used. First and second type Riviera front
wheel cylinders can be identified by the size cast into each wheel
cylinder casting. See illustration. It is important that both front
wheel cylinders be of the same size, therefore, when servicing
Riviera front wheel cylinders, be sure to install the correct repair
kit or wheel cylinder.

Listed below are the correct part numbers for first and second type
wheel cylinder assemblies and repair kits. Individual wheel cylinder
internal parts are listed in groups 4.667, 4.668 and 4.670.

FIRST TYPE (1-1/8" diameter)

4.665 - 5465043 R - 042L Cylinder
4.667 - 5455856   Repair Kit

SECOND TYPE (1-3/16" diameter)

4.665 - 5462121 R - 120L Cylinder
4.667 - 5456566   Repair Kit

Service Department
BUICK MOTOR DIVISION

DATE: April 20, 1967

SUBJECT: 1967 Buick and Opel Dealer Installed
            Accessories Applicable to 1968 Models

For your information and guidance in controlling your
inventory of 1967 Buick and Opel accessories, we are
furnishing the attached listing of 1967 model accessories applicable to 1968 models. Also shown are 1967
accessories not applicable to 1968 models.

This information should be helpful to you in maintaining
an adequate supply of 1967 Buick and Opel accessories
throughout the model year.

The attached listings were developed in accordance with
information available at this time. Any changes to the
listings will be furnished you at the earliest possible
date.

Parts and Accessories

Merchandising Department

Group	Part No.	Description	Model Application
2.485	981182	Twilight Sentinel	Upper Series
2.774	980702	Courtesy Light	All Models
2.810	981278	Four Note Horn	LeSabre, Wildcat, Electra
3.028	980879	Locking Gas Tank Cap	All Models
5.858	980787	Wheel Cover Wire 14" W/Spinner	Special, Sport Wagon,
5.858	980788	Wheel Cover Wire 15" W/Spinner	LeSabre
5.858	980789	Wheel Cover Wire 15" W/Spinner	Riviera
5.858	981283	Wheel Cover Wire 15" W/O Spinner	Wildcat
5.858	981199	Wheel Cover Super Deluxe	Riviera
5.858	981270	Wheel Cover Wire 14" W/O Spinner	Special, Skylark, Sport Wagon, GS-400
5.858	981271	Wheel Cover Wire 15" W/O Spinner	LeSabre
7.068	980670	Trailer Hitch Ball 2"	All Models
7.068	981148	Trailer Hitch Ball 1 7/8"	All Models
7.068	981256	Trailer Hitch	LeSabre, Wildcat, Electra
7.675	981048	Spare Tire Lock	All Models
8.800	987570	Polishing Cloth	All Models
8.821	986792	Highway Emergency Kit	All Models
8.873	981247	Compass	All Models
8.891	980234	Litter Basket - Black	All Models
8.891	980667	Litter Basket - Red	All Models
8.891	980668	Litter Basket - Blue	All Models
8.891	980669	Litter Basket - Beige	All Models
8.892	980590	Purse Hook	All Models
9.551	980842	Cushion Topper - Black Front	Upper Series 4-Door
9.551	980843	Cushion Topper - Blue Front	Upper Series 4-Door
9.551	980845	Cushion Topper - Fawn Front	Upper Series 4-Door
9.551	980846	Cushion Topper - Red Front	Upper Series 4-Door
9.551	980847	Cushion Topper - Gray Front	Upper Series 4-Door
9.551	980854	Cushion Topper - Black Front	Upper Series 2-Door
9.551	980855	Cushion Topper - Blue Front	Upper Series 2-Door
9.551	980857	Cushion Topper - Fawn Front	Upper Series 2-Door
9.551	980858	Cushion Topper - Red Front	Upper Series 2-Door
9.551	980859	Cushion Topper - Gray Front	Upper Series 2-Door
9.551	981020	Cushion Topper - Green Front	Upper Series 4-Door
9.551	981021	Cushion Topper - Green Front	Upper Series 2-Door
9.551	981022	Cushion Topper - Black Rear	Upper Series 4-Door
9.551	981023	Cushion Topper - Blue Rear	Upper Series 4-Door
9.551	981024	Cushion Topper - Green Rear	Upper Series 4-Door
9.551	981025	Cushion Topper - Fawn Rear	Upper Series 4-Door
9.551	981026	Cushion Topper - Red Rear	Upper Series 4-Door
9.551	981027	Cushion Topper - Gray Rear	Upper Series 4-Door
9.560	980731	Salesman Desk	All Models
9.560	981135	Kar Porta Desk	All Models except long console
9.645	981098	Antenna-Manual	Riviera
9.645	981211	Antenna - Manual	LeSabre, Wildcat, Electra
9.773	981130	Spot Lamp - Remote Control	All Except Riviera

1

Group	Part No.	Description	Model Application
9.777	981966	License Plate Frame	All Models
9.988	980718	Luggage Compartment Light	Special, Skylark, GS-400
9.988	981201	Utility Light - Hood or Trunk	All Models
9.988	981277	Trunk Light	Upper Series
9.990	985592	Fire Extinguisher	All Models
9.990	985593	Fire Extinguisher - Refill	All Models
10.195	981274	Vanity Mirror - Visor	All Models
10.275	980826	Glove Compartment & Ash Tray Light	Special
10.352	981230	Door Edge Guards	LeSabre, Wildcat, Electra-2-Door
10.352	981231	Door Edge Guards	LeSabre, Wildcat, Electra-4-Door
10.352	981232	Door Edge Guards	Riviera
12.243	981248	Automatic Trunk Release	Special, Skylark, GS-400
12.243	981275	Automatic Trunk Release	LeSabre, Wildcat, Electra
12.800	980723	Station Wagon Pad-Charcoal & Blue	Special Wagon, Sport Wagon
12.800	980724	Station Wagon Pad-Red & Yellow	Special Wagon, Sport Wagon
12.800	981128	Pad-Station Wagon	Special Wagon, Sport Wagon
12.800	981191	Mat--Station Wagon	Special and Sport Wagon
12.815	980482	Kar Pak Luggage Carrier	All Models Except Convertible & Wagons W/carriers
12.815	980495	Kar Pak Luggage Carrier	All Models -exc Convert.& Wagons W/carrier.)
12.815	981195	Ski Rack	All Models
14.875	980883	Seat Belt Retractor	All Models
15.292	980958	Mat - Front Overall-Black	LeSabre, Wildcat, Electra
15.292	980963	Mat - Front Overall-Fawn	LeSabre, Wildcat, Electra
15.292	980993	Mat - Handy - Fawn	All Models
15.292	980997	Mat - Handy - Black	All Models
15.292	980998	Carpet Saver - Black	All Models
15.292	981000	Carpet Saver - Fawn	All Models
15.292	981004	Mat - Front Overall - Black	Special, Skylark, Sport Wagon GS-400
15.292	981006	Mat - Front Overall - Fawn	Special, Skylark, Sport Wagon GS-400
15.292	981010	Mat - Rear Overall - Black	All Models Except Riviera
15.292	981012	Mat - Rear Overall - Fawn	All Models Except Riviera
15.294	980219	Mat - Trunk	All Models Except Convertibles and Wagons
15.388	980595	Clothes Rod	All Models Except Convertibles

P & A Merchandising
   4-20-67

2

9 7

Group	Part No.	Description	Model Application
0.003	981268	Engine Dress-up Kit	Wildcat GS-400-Electra-Riviera W/AIR
0.003	981269	Engine Dress-up Kit	GS-400-Wildcat-Electra-Riviera
0.034	980603	Engine Block Heater	Wildcat-Electra-Riviera-GS-400
0.034	981139	Engine Block Heater	Special-Skylark-LeSabre
2.459	981236	Guide-Matic Headlight Control	All Models
2.585	981249	Cornering Lamp	LeSabre-Wildcat-Electra (except tilt wheel jobs).
2.585	981250	Cornering Lamp	Riviera
2.585	981280	Cornering Lamp	LeSabre-Wildcat-Electra (Tilt Wheel Jobs)
2.774	981138	Courtesy Lamp	LeSabre-Wildcat (Electra Standard
5.858	981196	Wheel Cover	Special-Skylark (Wagon-Standard)
5.858	981197	Wheel Cover	Skylark (exc. Sport Wagon)
5.858	981198	Wheel Cover	LeSabre-Super Deluxe. (Electra Standard)
5.858	981203	Wheel Cover	Special-Skylark-Sport Wagon-LeSabre-GS-400 15" Wheels
5.858	981204	Wheel Cover - Standard	Wildcat
5.858	981205	Wheel Cover - Standard	Riviera
6.508	981207	Power Steering Package	GS-400
6.508	981208	Power Steering Package	Special-Skylark exc. GS-400
6.508	981209	Power Steering Package	LeSabre
6.508	981210	Power Steering Package	Wildcat
6.518	981258	Tilt Steering Wheel Pkg.	Special & Skylark A.T.
6.518	981259	Tilt Steering Wheel Pkg.	LeSabre-Wildcat-Electra A.T. & P.S. exc. console shift.
6.518	981260	Tilt Steering Wheel Pkg.	Wildcat A.T. & P.S. console shift
7.068	981129	Trailer Hitch	Riviera
7.068	981132	Trailer Hitch	Sport Wagon
7.068	981133	Trailer Hitch	Electra
7.068	981150	Trailer Hitch	Special Wagons
7.068	981255	Trailer Hitch	Special & Skylark exc wagons
7.068	980893	Trailer Wiring Harness	Special-Skylark-GS-400 Electra - Riviera
7.068	981272	Trailer Wiring Harness	Special & Sport Wagon
7.068	981279	Trailer Wiring Harness	LeSabre - Wildcat
7.345	981239	Automatic Level Control	LeSabre
7.345	981240	Automatic Level Control	Wildcat - Electra
7.345	981241	Automatic Level Control	Riviera
7.345	981242	Automatic Level Control	Sport Wagon
8.210	981100	Gas Tank Door Guard	Wagons
8.891	980820	Tissue Dispenser	All exc. Special & Skylark W/Air Conditioning
9.169	981246	Custom Air Conditioner	Special-Skylark-Sport Wagon
9.169	981243	Four Seasons Air Conditioner	LeSabre-Wildcat-Electra
9.169	981244	A/C attaching Parts Pkg.	LeSabre
9.169	981245	A/C attaching Parts Pkg.	Wildcat - Electra

3

1967 BUICK DEALER INSTALLED ACCESSORIES NOT APPLICABLE TO 1968 MODELS

Group	Part No.	Description	Model Application
9.645	981096	Antenna-Manual	Special and Skylark
9.645	981212	Antenna-Electric	LeSabre-Wildcat-Electra
9.645	981215	Antenna-Electric	Riviera
9.650	981184	Radio-Sonomatic	Special-Skylark-Sport Wagon GS-400
9.650	981186	Radio Sonomatic	LeSabre-Wildcat-Electra
9.650	981229	Radio Sonomatic	Riviera
9.650	981185	Radio - AM-FM	Special and Skylark
9.650	981187	Radio - AM-FM	LeSabre-Wildcat - Electra
9.650	981189	Radio - AM-FM	Riviera
9.650	981188	Radio - AM-FM Stereo	LeSabre-Wildcat-Electra
9.650	981190	Radio - AM-FM Stereo	Riviera
9.665	981192	Rear Seat Speaker	LeSabre - Wildcat - Electra
9.665	981193	Rear Seat Speaker	Riviera
9.665	981194	Rear Seat Speaker	Special - Skylark - GS-400- Sport Wagon exc convertible
9.665	980869	Reverberator - tone	All exc. Special - Skylark convertible
9.670**	981284	Bracket Pkg. Stereo Tape Player	Special-Skylark-Sport Wagon - GS-400
9.772	981216	Clock	Special and Skylark
9.772	981091	Clock	LeSabre-Wildcat (Electra-Std.)
9.777	980182	License Plate Frame	LeSabre-Wildcat-Electra
9.778	981106	Defroster - Rear Window	LeSabre-Wildcat - Electra - except Convertible
9.778	981127	Defroster - Rear Window	Riviera
9.778	981206	Defroster - Rear Window	Special & Skylark exc. convt. Wagons
10.185	981257	Mirror - Outside Rear View - Manual	All Models
10.185	981016	Mirror Remote Control	All Models
10.352	981233	Door Edge Guards	Special - Skylark - GS-400 2-Door
10.352	981234	Door Edge Guards	Special-Skylark-Sport Wagon - 4-Door
10.559	981254	Door Lock Guards	All Models
12.180	981044	Custom Air Deflector	Special and Sport Wagons
12.243	981108	Automatic Trunk Lid Release	Riviera
12.815	980828	Kar Pak Luggage Carrier	Special Wagons W/Roof carrier
12.815	980909	Kar Pak Luggage Carrier	Sport Wagon W/Roof carrier
12.815	980986	Ski Rack & Luggage Carrier	Wagons W/Roof carrier
12.815	980811	Roof Top Carrier-Luggage	Special Wagons
12.815	980908	Roof Top Carrier-Luggage	Sport Wagon
15.292	980999	Carpet Savers - Blue	All Models
15.292	981001	Carpet Savers - Green	All Models
15.292	981002	Carpet Savers - Red	All Models
15.292	981113	Carpet Savers - Aqua	All Models
15.292	980961	Carpet Covers - Green	LeSabre - Wildcat - Electra
9.670	981285	Stereo Tape Player	All Models exc Long Console

4

Group	Part No.	Description	Model Application
15.292	980962	Carpet Covers - Blue	LeSabre - Wildcat - Electra
15.292	980965	Carpet Covers - Red	LeSabre - Wildcat - Electra
15.292	981111	Carpet Covers - Aqua	LeSabre - Wildcat - Electra
15.292	981005	Carpet Covers - Blue	Special and Skylark
15.292	981007	Carpet Covers - Green	Special and Skylark
15.292	981008	Carpet Covers - Red	Special and Skylark
15.292	981112	Carpet Covers - Aqua	Special and Skylark
15.292	980991	Handy Mats - Green	All Models
15.292	980992	Handy Mats - Blue	All Models
15.292	980995	Handy Mats - Red	All Models
15.292	981110	Handy Mats - Aqua	All Models
15.292	981011	Rear Overall Mats - Blue	All except Riviera
15.292	981013	Rear Overall Mats - Green	All except Riviera
15.292	981014	Rear Overall Mats - Red	All except Riviera
15.292	981109	Rear Overall Mats - Aqua	All except Riviera

1967 OPEL KADETT DEALER INSTALLED ACCESSORIES APPLICABLE TO 1968 MODELS

Group	Part No.	Description	Model Application
2.810	981145	Dual Horn	All Models
3.705	981297	Tail Pipe Extension	All Models
5.858	981146	Wheel Trim Rings	All Models
5.858	981155	Wire Wheel Cover	All Models
7.068	980670	Ball, Trailer Hitch 2"	All Models
7.068	981148	Ball, Trailer Hitch 1 7/8"	All Models
7.068	981180	Trailer Hitch	Wagons
7.628	981289	Spare Tire Storage Parts Pkg	All Except Wagons
7.628	981290	Spare Tire Storage Pts Pkg	Wagons
8.821	986792	Highway Emergency Kit	All Models
8.873	981247	Compass	All Models
9.645	981947	Antenna	All Models
9.772	981144	Clock	All Models
9.990	985592	Fire Extinguisher	All Models
9.990	985593	Fire Extinguisher Refill Kit	All Models
10.352	981295	Door Edge Guards	All Models
12.045	980889	Ash Tray - Rear Quarter	All Models
12.815	980482	Kar Pak Luggage Carrier	All Except Wagons
13.347	981238	Custom Vinyl Roof Covering	Sport Coupe
14.875	980883	Seat Belt Retractor	All Models
15.292	981202	Carpet Savers	All Models
15.294	980219	Station Wagon Mat	Wagons

1967 OPEL KADETT DEALER INSTALLED ACCESSORIES NOT APPLICABLE TO 1968 MODELS

Group	Part No.	Description	Model Application
7.068	981147	Trailer Hitch	All Except Wagons
8.891	980820	Tissue Dispenser	All Models
9.650	981263	Radio	All Models
9.777	980182	Frame, License Plate	All Models
10.185	981016	Mirror, Remote Control	All Models
10.275	981163	Glove Box Light	All Models
12.007	981262	Cigar Lighter	All Models
12.815	980909	Kar Pak Luggage Carrier	Wagons W/carriers

Parts and Accessories
Merchandising Department

4-20-67

CHAPTER FIVE

1968 RIVIERA

INFORMATION BULLETIN NUMBER		DEALER FILE	
		Model Year	1968
68-I-43		File in Group	60
		Number	5

BUICK DEALER
SERVICE INFORMATION
BULLETIN

BUICK MOTOR DIVISION • **GENERAL MOTORS CORPORATION** • **FLINT, MICHIGAN 48550**

December 29, 1967

TO ALL BUICK DEALERS

SUBJECT: 1968 Buick Engine Identification and 1967 and 1968 Foreign Travel Information

Listed on Chart A are the various engines used in the 1968 Buick Automobiles.

Owners contemplating travel outside the United States should be cautioned to check on the quality of fuel available before their trip. For your convenience, the engine chart will serve as a guide in determining engine identification, compression ratio, fuel octane requirements, etc. Zone Service and Parts Managers have a publication listing the octanes of the fuels found in most countries of the world.

With the 1968 Olympic Games being held in Mexico, it can be assured many domestic vehicles will be traveling to the event. To compensate for the available premium fuel which varies between 90 and 100 octane, Engineering has released parts to reduce engine detonation. They include a .045" thick head gasket for reduction in compression ratio and a set of distributor springs to modify ignition timing. Refer to Chart B for the correct gasket and distributor spring part number.

Light detonation may still be encountered in some instances, however; it is not considered injurious to the engine. It is suggested that the distributor springs be removed when the vehicle returns from Mexico. The head gasket may be removed at the owners discretion as leaving them in the engine would result in a slight loss of fuel economy.

If satisfactory fuels cannot be assured, the compression ratio should be lowered by installing export pistons as indicated on Chart B.

NOTE: Engine damage caused by detonation as a result of the use of low octane fuels is not considered a defect in material or workmanship; therefore, cannot be considered for warranty adjustment.

Service Department
BUICK MOTOR DIVISION
Flint, Michigan

gine Mfg. Code mber Prefix	Engine Description & Carburetor Equipment	Compression Ratio	Octane Requirement	Horsepower at RPM
*	250 cu.in. L-6- 1 barrel	8.5 to 1	93 Research	155 at 4200
*	250 cu.in. L-6- 1 barrel (export low compression)	7.25 to 1	81 Research	136 at 4000
PO	350 cu.in. V-8 - 2 barrel	9.0 to 1	93 Research	230 at 4400
PP	350 cu.in. V-8 - 4 barrel	10.25 to 1	99 Research	280 at 4600
PW	350 cu.in. V-8 - 2 barrel (export low compression)	8.1 to 1	85 Research	225 at 4400
PR	400 cu.in. V-8 - 4 barrel	10.25 to 1	99 Research	340 at 5000
PD	430 cu.in. V-8 - 4 barrel	10.25 to 1	99 Research	360 at 5000
PE	430 cu.in. V-8 - 4 barrel (export low compression)	8.75 to 1	93 Research	330 at 5000

* The L-6 will carry Chevrolet's method of identification

Example	F	12	07	SA
	Plant	Month	Day	Engine

105

CHART B

Available Research Octane Number and Recommended Parts to Install in Distributor and/or Engine

Engine	98 - 100	94 - 98	90 - 94	86 - 90	82 - 86
1967 - 400 & 430 Cu.In. Engine - 10.25:1 Compression Ratio	As Released	Dist. Springs #1886538	Dist. Springs #1886538 Head Gaskets #1384094	Dist.Springs #1886538 Head Gaskets #1384094	*Export Pistons 430 Cu.In. #1395653
1967 - 300 & 340 Cu.In. Engine - 4 bbl. - 10.25:1 Compression Ratio	As Released	Dist. Springs #1933350 (340 Cu.In.) / Dist. Springs #1917710 (300 Cu.In.)	Dist. Springs #1933350 (340 Cu.In.) / Dist. Springs #1917710 (300 Cu.In.) / Head Gaskets #1379757	Export Pistons #1395513	Export Pistons #1395513
1967 - 300 & 340 Cu.In. Engine - 2 bbl. 9.0:1 Compression Ratio	As Released	As Released	As Released	Dist.Springs #1933350 (340 Cu.In.) Dist.Spgs. #1917710 (300 Cu.In.) Head Gaskets #1379757	Export Pistons #1395513
1967 - 225 Cu.In. Engine - 2 bbl. 9 0:1 Compression Ratio	As Released	As Released	As Released	Dist.Springs #1933350 Head Gaskets #1384256	Export Pistons #1395513
1968 - 400 & 430 Cu.In. Engine - 10.25:1 Compression Ratio	As Released	Dist. Springs #1970823	Dist. Springs #1970823 Head Gaskets	Dist.Springs #1970823 Head Gaskets #1384094	*Export Pistons 430 Cu.In. #1395653
1968 - 350 Cu.In. Engine - 4 bbl. 10.25:1 Compression Ratio	As Released	Dist. Springs #1933350	Dist. Springs #1933350 Head Gaskets	Dist.Springs #1933350 Head Gaskets #1385204	Export Pistons #1396206
1968 - 350 Cu.In. Engine - 2 bbl. 9.0:1 Compression Ratio	As Released	As Released	As Released	Dist.Springs #1971709 Head Gaskets #1385204	Export Pistons #1394206
1968 - 250 Cu.In. Engine - 1 bbl. 8.5:1 Compression Ratio	As Released	As Released	As Released	Export Pistons #3886055	Export Pistons #3886055

NOTE: If spark rap is encountered after the above appropriate modifications have been incorporated, the ignition timing may be retarded 2½° to correct the problem temporarily.

* Export pistons are not available for the 400 Cu. In. engines.

BUICK DEALER
SERVICE INFORMATION
BULLETIN

BUICK MOTOR DIVISION • GENERAL MOTORS CORPORATION • FLINT, MICHIGAN 48550

September 15, 1967

SUBJECT: Serializing 1968 Engine and Transmission Assemblies,
Engine Blocks and Transmission Cases

You will note in the 1968 Owner's Manuals that a great deal of
emphasis is placed on anti-theft information as well as safety.
To aid law enforcement agencies, Buick Motor Division will stamp
on engine and transmission assemblies the last digits of the vehicle
identification number. See illustration. General Motors Assembly
Division produced cars will have the engine and transmission
assemblies stamped with the Number 4 preceeding the last eight
(8) digits of the vehicle identification number. (Number 4
signifies Buick Motor Division.) Flint produced units will use
the last eight (8) digits of the vehicle identification number.

Service engine and transmission assemblies, as well as transmission
cases and engine blocks obtained through the Parts Department, will
also have numbers stamped in the space provided at the various
locations shown in the attached illustration. These numbers are
provided on replacement assemblies so that they may be appropriately
recorded at the dealership to comply with any existing state legislation. Numbers on replacement units are not to be altered.

Replacement numbers will differ from the vehicle identification
number so that it can be determined that a replacement assembly
was used.

This information is being provided you so that you may comply with
any existing legislation which makes it mandatory that records be
maintained to show proof that replacement assemblies were installed.

Service Department
BUICK MOTOR DIVISION

250 CU. IN. L-6

350 CU. IN.

400 & 430 CU. IN.

1968 ENGINE SERIAL NUMBER LOCATIONS

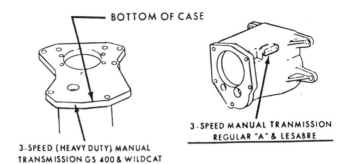

BOTTOM OF CASE

3-SPEED (HEAVY DUTY) MANUAL
TRANSMISSION GS 400 & WILDCAT

3-SPEED MANUAL TRANMISSION
REGULAR "A" & LESABRE

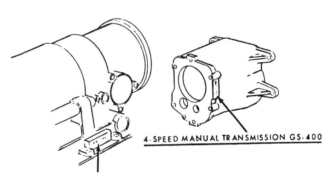

ST-300 & ST-400 AUTOMATIC TRANSMISSION

4-SPEED MANUAL TRANSMISSION GS-400

1968 TRANSMISSION SERIAL NUMBER LOCATIONS

BUICK MOTOR DIVISION • GENERAL MOTORS CORPORATION • FLINT, MICHIGAN 48550

TO ALL BUICK DEALERS

January 26, 1968

SUBJECT: Oil Economy

We have received dealer requests for information pertaining to normal oil economy in today's engines. What is normal oil comsumption can best be answered if specific driving conditions to which a car is subjected are known. It is similar to asking, what is the normal fuel economy for any given model. If there were not so many variables involved, a simple specific statement could be offered.

The information below is in agreement with our Engineering Department, and since it is a down-to-earth reply we are hopeful that it will be useful in handling owners' inquiries on oil consumption.

"A gasoline engine depends upon oil to lubricate the cylinder walls, pistons, and piston rings. When the piston moves downward, a thin film of oil is left on the cylinder walls, and on the firing stroke it is burned by the flame of combustion. If an engine burned as much as one drop of oil on every firing stroke, then it would use more than a quart every two miles. Such consumption is unheard of in the automotive field, but all efficient engines use some oil. If they did not, they would quickly wear out.

The rate of consumption depends upon the quality and viscosity of the oil, the speed at which the engine is operated, the temperature and the amount of dilution and oxidation which takes place. These conditions are frequently misleading. As an example, a car that has run 1000 miles or more in city operation, may have consumed a normal amount of oil, yet actually measures up to the full mark due to dilution in the crankcase. The car then might be driven at high speed on the highway, the dilution elements boil off rapidly, and the car appears to use two quarts of oil in a hundred miles.

Car owners should expect increased oil consumption at high speeds. For instance, it is a proven fact that an automotive engine may use seven times the quantity of oil at 70 than it will at 40 miles per hour. No standard rate of consumption can be established because under various combinations of the conditions mentioned above, one engine might use a quart in 1,500 miles and another use a quart in 750 miles and yet both engines might be entirely normal.

New engines require considerable running before the piston rings and cylinder walls become 'conditioned', and during this time they use oil more rapidly than later. An engine's oil economy should not be judged until it has run at least 4000 miles."

Keeping the above information in mind be certain that the owner is using the oil recommended in the owners guide. It is extremely important to use the correct viscosity oil for the climate condition encountered by the car. Also, that the oil container be labeled for service MS, passes car makers' tests or meets General Motors Standard GM 6041-M.

Service Department
BUICK MOTOR DIVISION
Flint, Michigan

BUICK MOTOR DIVISION
1968 AXLE RATIOS

SERIES	ENGINES	AUTOMATIC TRANSMISSIONS				MANUAL TRANSMISSIONS			
		Standard	Economy	Performance	Special Car Order(A)	Standard	Economy	Performance	Special Car Order(A)
SPECIAL DELUXE Coupe & Sedan	Fireball 250-1 6	2.93	NA	3.23	3.42 3.91	3.23	NA	NA	3.91
	Fireball 250-1 6 w/AC	3.23	NA	3.42	NA	3.23	NA	NA	3.91
	Wildcat 350-2 V8	2.56	NA	3.23	3.91	2.93	NA	NA	3.91
	Wildcat 350-2 V8 w/AC	2.73	NA	3.23	3.91	NA	NA	NA	NA
	Wildcat 350-4 V8	2.73	NA	3.23	3.91	2.93	NA	NA	3.91
SPECIAL DELUXE Wagon	Wildcat 350-2 V8	2.93	2.73	3.23	3.91	2.93	NA	NA	3.91
	Wildcat 350-4 V8	2.73	2.73	3.23	3.91	2.93	NA	NA	3.91
GS 350	Wildcat 350-4 V8	3.23	NA	3.42	NA	3.23	NA	3.42	3.64
SKYLARK	Fireball 250-1 6	2.93	NA	3.23	3.42 3.91	3.23	NA	NA	3.91
	Fireball 250-1 6 w/AC	3.23	NA	3.42	3.91	3.23	NA	NA	3.91
	Wildcat 350-2 V8	2.56	NA	3.23	3.91	2.93	NA	NA	3.91
	Wildcat 350-2 V8 w/AC	2.73	NA	3.23	3.91	2.93	NA	NA	NA
	Wildcat 350-4 V8	2.73	2.56	3.23	3.91	2.93	NA	NA	3.91
SKYLARK CUSTOM	Wildcat 350-2 V8	2.73	2.56	3.23	3.91	2.93	NA	NA	3.42 3.91
	Wildcat 350-2 V8 w/AC	2.73	NA	3.23	3.91	2.93	NA	NA	3.42 3.91
	Wildcat 350-4 V8	2.73	2.56	3.23	3.42 3.91	2.93	NA	NA	3.42 3.91
GS 400	Wildcat 400-4 V8	2.93	2.56	3.42	3.64 3.91	3.42	NA	3.64 PT / NA NON PT	3.91
SPORTWAGON	Wildcat 350-2 V8	3.23	2.93	3.42	3.64 3.91	3.23	NA	NA	3.91
	Wildcat 350-4 V8	3.23	2.93	3.42	3.64 3.91	3.23	NA	NA	3.91
SPORTWAGON 400 (Opt.)	Wildcat 400-4 V8	3.23	2.93	3.42	3.42 3.91	NA	NA	NA	NA
LeSABRE	Wildcat 350-2 V8	2.93	2.73(B)	3.42	3.42 3.91	3.23	NA	NA	3.91
	Wildcat 350-4 V8	2.93	2.93	3.42	3.91	3.23	NA	NA	3.91
WILDCAT	Wildcat 430-4 V8	3.07	2.78	3.42 PT / 3.23 NON PT	3.91	3.07	NA	NA	NA
ELECTRA 225	Wildcat 430-4 V8	2.78	2.56	3.23	3.91	NA	NA	NA	NA
RIVIERA	Wildcat 430-4 V8	3.07	NA	3.42 PT / 3.23 NON PT	3.91	NA	NA	NA	NA
RIVIERA GS (Option)	Wildcat 430-4 V8	3.42 PT	NA	NA	NA	NA	NA	NA	NA

(A) All special car order ratios are available only with positive traction.
(B) Not available with air conditioner.

w/AC—with air conditioner.   NA—not available.   PT—positive traction.

BUICK DEALER
SERVICE TECHNICAL
BULLETIN

BUICK MOTOR DIVISION • GENERAL MOTORS CORPORATION • FLINT, MICHIGAN 48550

October 4, 1968

TO ALL BUICK DEALERS

SUBJECT: Use of Composition Head Gaskets On 1968 400 and 430 Cu. In. Engines

REISSUED TO REVISE INFORMATION ON CYLINDER HEAD BOLT TORQUE

400 and 430 cu. in. engines with PD-600, 700, 800 or 900 series code numbers have been built with a .045" composition head gasket on both banks.

If service replacement is required on the composition head gaskets, it is of the utmost importance that composition gaskets be used for replacement.

If a steel cylinder head gasket is removed due to a coolant leak on a 1968 350, 400, or 430 cu. in. engine, it is recommended that a composition gasket be used.

When using composition cylinder head gaskets, torque cylinder bolts in the sequence shown in Figure 1 and to the following torque:

Engine	Torque
400, 430 Cu. In.	100 lbs. ft.
350 Cu. In.	80 lbs. ft.

NOTE: It is not necessary to install a composition gasket on both heads when replacing a steel gasket as this will not affect engine operation. Only replace gasket that is leaking.

Composition head gaskets are available as follows:

Engine	Group	Part Number	Dealer Price
350	0.289	1385204	$2.25
400-430	0.289	1384094	$1.91

Service Department
BUICK MOTOR DIVISION
Flint, Michigan

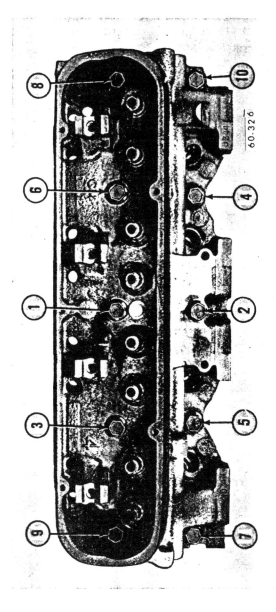

60-326

FIGURE 1

BUICK DEALER
SERVICE INFORMATION
BULLETIN

BUICK MOTOR DIVISION • GENERAL MOTORS CORPORATION • FLINT, MICHIGAN 48550

October 4, 1967

TO ALL BUICK DEALERS

SUBJECT: 1968 4MV Quadrajet Carburetor - Timing, Idle Speed, Mixture and Fast Idle Adjustments

On all 1968 4MV Quadrajet Carburetors, it will be necessary to check and adjust timing, idle speed, mixture and fast idle, as part of new car pre-delivery service as described below.

IMPORTANT: When making timing, idle speed, mixture and fast idle adjustment, temporarily disconnect distributor vacuum line at distributor and plug line while following adjustments are being made.

NOTE: The vacuum hose must be removed at the distributor and plugged so the thermo vacuum switch can not switch the distributor over to full vacuum advance if coolant temperature should rise above 220° F. (switch is calibrated at 220° F.)

CAUTION: <u>Under no circumstances should the vacuum line be disconnected at any location other than the distributor.</u>

1. With engine idling and vacuum hose disconnected at distributor, plug line and set timing at 0° T.D.C. for all 8 cylinder engines except 400 cu. in. manual transmission equipped vehicles. 400 cu. in. manual transmission equipped vehicles are to be timed at $2\frac{1}{2}^\circ$ after T.D.C.

2. Idle speed and mixture adjustments must be made before fast idle adjustment is made and must be done as follows:

NOTE: The air cleaner must be left in place while making idle speed and mixture adjustments. The positive crankcase ventilator system should be in good operating condition when making carburetor adjustments.

    a. Connect an accurate tachometer to engine.

    b. Start engine and run at fast idle until upper radiator hose is hot and choke valve is wide open.

CAUTION: Idle speed and mixture adjustments cannot be made satisfactorily with an abnormally hot engine. It is very important that idle adjustments be made at normal temperature so that the hot idle compensator valve and thermo vacuum switch will be in normal position.

    c. On automatic transmission cars, place a block in front of a wheel and apply parking brake firmly, then place transmission selector lever in Drive - "D".

NOTE: On Air Conditioner equipped cars, the air conditioner <u>MUST</u> <u>BE</u> <u>OFF</u>.

CAUTION: Any car which is equipped with Automatic Level Control has a vacuum regulator valve which shuts off all vacuum to the air compressor during engine idle, thereby preventing the compressor from operating and upsetting engine idle. Feel compressor with hand, to make certain it is not operating. If it is operating refer to Group 40, Section B paragraph 45-10, Subparagraph B, of the 1968 Chassis Service Manual.

    d. Adjust throttle stop screw to set idle speed according to specifications listed below:

350 Eng. - Manual transmission	700 RPM
350 Eng. - Automatic transmission	550 RPM
400 Eng. - Manual transmission	700 RPM
400 Eng. - Automatic transmission	600 RPM
430 Eng. - Automatic transmission	550 RPM

    e. Adjust idle mixture needles, one at a time, to obtain highest reading. After highest reading is reached using mixture needles, readjust throttle stop screw as required to obtain 20 RPM faster than specified idle. Next, turn <u>each</u> mixture needle in (lean) as required to reduce engine speed 10 RPM (for total loss of 20 RPM). This reduces idle speed to the recommended idle RPM.

NOTE: This method of adjusting idle mixture <u>must be used</u> to keep hydrocarbon and carbon monoxide emissions to a minimum.

3. Shift air cleaner to the left to obtain access to the fast idle cam. Fast idle adjustment must be set with engine warm transmission in drive and cam follower on <u>low</u> step of fast idle cam. Adjust fast idle screw so that engine runs 20 RPM faster than specified idle speed. See illustration. Re-position air cleaner and connect vacuum line to distributor. It is essential that fast idle adjustment be made as it affects cold start, false starts, and general driveability during warm up.

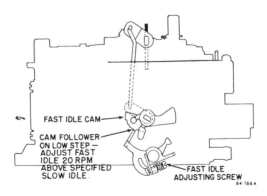

FAST IDLE CAM

CAM FOLLOWER
ON LOW STEP -
ADJUST FAST
IDLE 20 RPM
ABOVE SPECIFIED
SLOW IDLE.

FAST IDLE
ADJUSTING SCREW

64-166A

BUICK DEALER
SERVICE TECHNICAL
BULLETIN

BUICK MOTOR DIVISION • GENERAL MOTORS CORPORATION • FLINT, MICHIGAN 48550

November 24, 1967

TO ALL BUICK DEALERS

SUBJECT: Stall After Start on 400 and 430 Cubic Inch Displacement Engines

A few Dealer Product Reports indicate that a stall after start exists on some 400 and 430 cubic inch displacement engines. To overcome this condition the vacuum break setting should be changed from .200" to .180".

To make the new setting proceed as follows: With the vacuum break diaphragm seated and with the vacuum break lever held upward lightly, the dimension between the lower edge of the choke valve and air horn should be .180". To adjust bend vacuum break tang, see illustration.

On 430 cubic inch displacement engines, this change went into production with change letter "B" stamped on the bowl. On 400 cubic inch displacement engines, the change went into production with change letter "A".

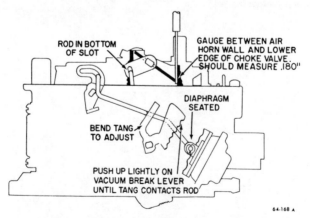

64-168 A

VACUUM BREAK ADJUSTMENT

Service Department
BUICK MOTOR DIVISION

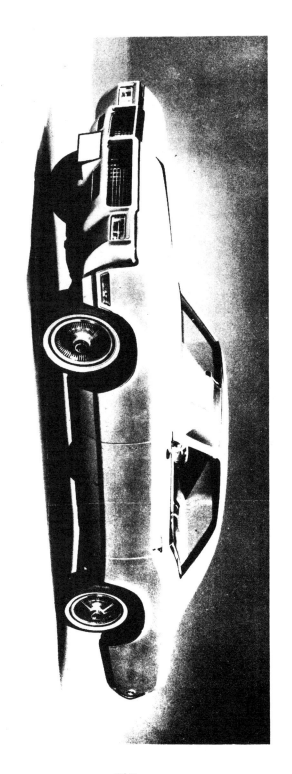

BUICK DEALER
SERVICE INFORMATION
BULLETIN

BUICK MOTOR DIVISION • **GENERAL MOTORS CORPORATION** • **FLINT, MICHIGAN 48550**

January 26, 1968

TO ALL BUICK DEALERS

SUBJECT: Positive Traction Clutch Pack Change – 1967 and 1968
46-48-49000 Series

A change has been made in the Positive Traction Clutch Pack
as used on 1967 and 1968 46-48-49000 series cars to reduce
the possibility of positive traction chatter. This new clutch
pack went into production on all axle ratios except 3.42 to 1
on June 1, 1967 and was carried over in 1968 models. On the
3.42 to 1 ratio, the new clutch pack did not go into production
until after Jobs 1968.

The new type 1967 and 1968 clutch pack has 6 external discs and
3 internal (friction) discs per side. See Figure 1. The early
type 1967 clutch pack has 5 external plates and 4 internal plates
per side. See Figure 2.

The service clutch pack, Gr. 5511, Part No. 1394261, Dealer Price
$12.00, has 8 external plates, 4 per side and 6 internal discs,
3 per side. When servicing any 1967 or 1968 46-48-49000 series
clutch with the service package, plates are to be installed as
shown in Figure 1. This will require using two of the original
external plates installed at the outboard side of each clutch pack.
See Figure 1. This information is also covered in the 1968
Service Manual.

NOTE: Never use chassis lube, wheel bearing grease or any type
of lube, other than recommended positive traction lube, to hold
clutch plates in place during assembly as a chatter complaint
will result.

Service Department
BUICK MOTOR DIVISION
Flint, Michigan

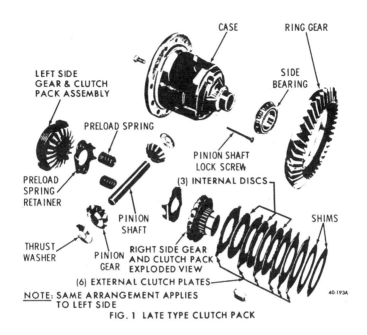

LEFT SIDE
GEAR & CLUTCH
PACK ASSEMBLY

CASE

RING GEAR

SIDE
BEARING

PRELOAD SPRING

PINION SHAFT
LOCK SCREW

PRELOAD
SPRING
RETAINER

(3) INTERNAL DISCS

SHIMS

PINION
SHAFT

THRUST
WASHER

PINION
GEAR

RIGHT SIDE GEAR
AND CLUTCH PACK
EXPLODED VIEW

(6) EXTERNAL CLUTCH PLATES

40-193A

NOTE: SAME ARRANGEMENT APPLIES
TO LEFT SIDE

FIG. 1 LATE TYPE CLUTCH PACK

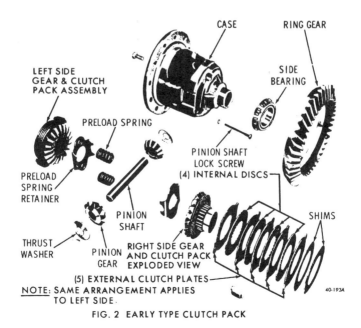

LEFT SIDE
GEAR & CLUTCH
PACK ASSEMBLY

CASE

RING GEAR

SIDE
BEARING

PRELOAD SPRING

PINION SHAFT
LOCK SCREW

PRELOAD
SPRING
RETAINER

(4) INTERNAL DISCS

SHIMS

PINION
SHAFT

THRUST
WASHER

PINION
GEAR

RIGHT SIDE GEAR
AND CLUTCH PACK
EXPLODED VIEW

(5) EXTERNAL CLUTCH PLATES

40-193A

NOTE: SAME ARRANGEMENT APPLIES
TO LEFT SIDE

FIG. 2 EARLY TYPE CLUTCH PACK

BUICK DEALER
SERVICE INFORMATION
BULLETIN

BUICK MOTOR DIVISION • GENERAL MOTORS CORPORATION • FLINT, MICHIGAN 48550

February 12, 1968

TO ALL BUICK DEALERS

SUBJECT: Out-Of-Round Brake Drums (Pulsating Brakes) - All 1968 Models

A recent investigation of pulsating brakes by factory personnel has revealed that driving habits of owners may be a contributing factor to pulsating brake complaints. The complaint we have in mind is one where the owner is unknowingly resting his foot against the brake thereby applying pressure to the hydraulic system sufficiently to energize the brake shoes against the brake drum. The drums have a tendency to become overheated when riding the pedal. Then, when the owner applies light pedal pressure in bringing his car to a stop, the pulsating effect becomes evident.

This has been demonstrated to owners and complaints have been handled without any repair work whatsoever. Therefore, we are requesting that all dealership service personnel be advised of the above condition and that no warranty work be performed without actually having an opportunity of riding the car with the owner to observe his driving habits.

Also, in the future, any drums that are to be turned will require zone authorization.

Service Department
BUICK MOTOR DIVISION

INFORMATION BULLETIN NUMBER
68-I-74

BUICK DEALER
SERVICE INFORMATION
BULLETIN

BUICK MOTOR DIVISION • **GENERAL MOTORS CORPORATION** • **FLINT, MICHIGAN 48550**

April 5, 1968

SUBJECT: Front Passenger Side Reclining Seat Back - All 1967 and 1968 Models Equipped With Optional Reclining Seat Back

Some reports have been received that the reclining seat back will not stay in a reclined position without an occupant in in the seat. Reports also indicate the reclining positioning units have been unnecessarily replaced for this complaint.

It should be noted that the operational specifications for the reclining seat back DO NOT require that the seat back must stay in a reclined position without an occupant in the seat, particularly if the head rest has been taken off the seat back.

Service Department
BUICK MOTOR DIVISION
Flint, Michigan

INFORMATION BULLETIN NUMBER		DEALER FILE	
		Model Year	**1968**
68-I-24		File in Group	68
		Number	1

BUICK DEALER
SERVICE INFORMATION
BULLETIN

BUICK MOTOR DIVISION • GENERAL MOTORS CORPORATION • FLINT, MICHIGAN 48550

November 10, 1967

Subject: a. 1968 Cruise Master Operation - First Jobs

b. 1968 Cruise Master Operation - After Jobs

a. 1968 Cruise Master Operation - First Jobs

The following information is being presented in an effort to clear up any confusion that may exist in the operation of the 1968 Cruise Master.

To more fully understand the operation of the Cruise Master switch, a certain characteristic should be recognized. The switch is labeled "OFF" and "ON". However, there is actually another "OFF" position. When the system is to be engaged and the switch is rotated toward "ON", the initial rotation engages the system. If the switch is rotated farther past "ON", the system becomes disengaged. Thus, a person rotating the switch fully to the stop and releasing it quickly may find the system not engaged. When this is done, the switch is moving too fast through "ON" toward the neutral (center) position not allowing the system to engage. Rotating it slowly back to neutral will insure engagement.

In the instructions below we have added the word, "slowly". These instructions may give a more clear presentation as to the operation of the 1968 Buick Cruise Master system.

To Engage:

1. Accelerate your car to the desired speed, using the accelerator pedal.

2. Rotate the "CRUISE CONTROL" switch to "ON" and release slowly. The cruise system is now engaged, as proven by the lighted cruise light.

   CAUTION: If the switch is allowed to snap back to its center position, the cruise system may not have time to engage.

To Re-Engage at a Faster Speed:

1. Accelerate to the newly desired faster speed, using the accelerator pedal.

2. Rotate the "CRUISE CONTROL" switch to "ON" and release <u>slowly</u>. The cruise system is now engaged at the new faster speed.

To Re-Engage at a Slower Speed:

1. Rotate the "CRUISE CONTROL" switch to "ON" and hold against the stop until the car decelerates to the newly desired slower speed.

2. At the instant the car reaches the new slower speed, release the "CRUISE CONTROL" switch <u>slowly</u>. The cruise system is now engaged at the new slower speed.

To Disengage:

1. Rotate the "CRUISE CONTROL" switch to "OFF", or

2. Apply the brake pedal, or

3. Turn off the ignition switch.

b. 1968 Cruise Master Operation - After Jobs

Due to the apparent confusion in the first type three-position switch, after-job Cruise Master systems will use a two-position switch which will simplify operation.

Operation for the new two-position switch is the same as first jobs, except there is no "OFF" position beyond the "ON" position. When you wish to re-engage the Cruise Master at a different speed, you must rotate switch to "OFF". When desired speed is reached, simply rotate switch to "ON" position.

NOTE: When the after-job Cruise Master system goes into production, a new light green instruction tag will accompany the system. Changes in Owner Manual text will be made in subsequent editions. Owners of after-job vehicles may have an Owner's Manual which applies to first-job switches. In these instances, however, it is felt that the revised instruction tag will provide sufficient instructions. Please have your Service Advisors and/or Owner Relations Manager informed of this change so they can answer owners' inquiries.

Service Department
BUICK MOTOR DIVISION

BUICK DEALER
SERVICE INFORMATION
BULLETIN

BUICK MOTOR DIVISION • **GENERAL MOTORS CORPORATION** • **FLINT, MICHIGAN 48550**

November 17, 1967

TO ALL BUICK DEALERS

SUBJECT: Special Paint Used On Textured Steel Mouldings With Fabric Roof Cover Option - 1968 Riviera

The exhaust grille on rear compartment front panel used on the 1968 Riviera requires special color to match the fabric roof cover material. Listed below are the paint colors available. The chart indicates the source and code numbers of released acrylic lacquer materials for field use.

Standard painting techniques should be followed when repainting.

COLOR	DuPONT Plus Flattening Compound #4528	R-M	DITZLER NO.
Parchment	9569L - *1-1/2 oz.	168V87	DDL or DIA 23034
Buckskin	9570L - *1-1/2 oz.	168V75	DDL or DIA 23036
Black	9333L - *2 oz.	168C41	DDL or DIA 9358
Avocado	9568L - *1-1/2 oz.	168V74	DDL or DIA 23035

* The amount of flattening compound (DuPont #4528) indicated should be added to one pint of unreduced color to arrive at the correct gloss level.

Service Department
BUICK MOTOR DIVISION

CHAPTER SIX

1969 RIVIERA

BUICK DEALER
SERVICE INFORMATION
BULLETIN

BUICK MOTOR DIVISION • GENERAL MOTORS CORPORATION • FLINT, MICHIGAN 48550

December 13, 1968

TO ALL BUICK DEALERS

SUBJECT: 1969 Buick Engine Identification and Foreign Travel
Information

Listed on Chart A are the various engines used in the 1969 Buick
Automobiles.

Owners anticipating travel outside the United States should be
cautioned that the fuels required for the 1969 domestic engines
must be of higher octane ratings than usually available outside
the continental limits of the United States and Canada. Since
low octane fuels will cause detonation which may seriously damage
the engine, modifications are recommended to reduce compression
ratio before foreign travel is attempted.

For your convenience, the engine chart will serve as a guide in
determining engine identification, compression ratio, fuel octane
requirements, etc. Zone Service and Parts Managers have a publication listing the octanes of the fuels found in most countries of
the world.

If satisfactory fuels cannot be assured, the information presented
on Chart B should be followed.

NOTE: Engine damage caused by detonation as a result of the use
of low octane fuels is not considered a defect in material
or workmanship; therefore, cannot be considered for warranty
adjustment.

> Service Department
> BUICK MOTOR DIVISION
> Flint, Michigan

CHART A

Engine Mfg. Code Number Prefix	Engine Description & Carburetor Equipment	Compression Ratio	Octane Requirement	Horsepower at RPM
*	250 cu.in. L-6 1 barrel	8.5 to 1	93 Research	155 at 4200
*	250 cu.in. L-6 1 barrel (export low compression)	7.25 to 1	81 Research	136 at 4000
RO	350 cu.in. V-8 2 barrel	9.0 to 1	93 Research	230 at 4400
RP	350 cu.in. V-8 4 barrel	10.25 to 1	99 Research	280 at 4600
RW	350 cu.in. V-8 2 barrel (export low compression)	8.0 to 1	85 Research	225 at 4400
RR	400 cu.in. V-8 4 barrel	10.25 to 1	99 Research	340 at 5000
RD	430 cu.in. V-8 4 barrel	10.25 to 1	99 Research	360 at 5000
RE	430 cu.in. V-8 4 barrel (export low compression)	8.75 to 1	93 Research	330 at 5000

* The L-6 will carry Chevrolet's method of identification.

EXAMPLE

F   12   07   SA

Plant   Month   Day   Engine

CHART B

Available Research Octane Number and Recommended Parts to Install in Distributor and/or Engine

ENGINE	98 - 100	94 - 98	90 - 94	86 - 90	82 - 86
1969-400 & 430 Cu.In.Eng. 10.25:1 Compression Ratio	As Released	Dist. Springs #1970823	Dist. Springs #1970823 Head Gaskets #1384094	Dist. Springs #1970823 Head Gaskets #1384094	*Export Pistons 430 Cu.In. #1395653
1969 - 350 Cu.In. Engine 4 bbl. 10.25:1 Compression Ratio	As Released	Dist. Springs #1933350	Dist. Springs #1933350 Head Gaskets #1385204	Export Pistons #1396206	Export Pistons #1396206
1969 - 350 Cu.In. Engine 2 bbl. 9.0:1 Compression Ratio	As Released	As Released	As Released	Dist. Springs #1971709 Head Gaskets #1385204	Export Pistons #1394206
1969 250 Cu.In. Engine 1 bbl. 8.5:1 Compression Ratio	As Released	As Released	As Released	Export Pistons #3886055	Export Pistons #3886055

NOTE: If spark rap is encountered after the above appropriate modifications have been incorporated, the ignition timing may be retarded $2\frac{1}{2}°$ to correct the problem temporarily.

* Export pistons are not available for the 400 Cu.In. engine.

BUICK DEALER
SERVICE INFORMATION
BULLETIN

BUICK MOTOR DIVISION • GENERAL MOTORS CORPORATION • FLINT, MICHIGAN 48550

December 13, 1968

TO ALL BUICK DEALERS

SUBJECT: 1969 Buick Paint Codes

Starting with 1969 production, Fisher Body Division utilizes number codes to identify the exterior paint color on the Body Identification Plate affixed to the body cowl.

Some of the assembly plants used this same paint number identification on the Vehicle Protect-O-Plates while others continued to use the letter designation. For uniformity all assembly plants will now use letters to identify paint color on the Vehicle Protect-O-Plate.

Service Department personnel will find the numbering system utilized on the car body plate and the paint color identification sheets distributed by Du Pont, Ditzler and Rinshed-Mason. Sales Department personnel will find the letter codes on sales literature, the new car order forms and on the Vehicle Protect-O-Plates.

1969 PAINT CODES

COLOR	SALES LETTER CODE	SERVICE NUMBER CODE
Regal Black	A	10
Burnished Brown	B	61
Polor White	C	50
Crystal Blue	D	53
Twilight Blue	E	51
Azure Blue	F	80
Trumpet Gold	G	65
Lime Green	H	59
Embassy Gold	J	75
Turquoise Mist	K	55
Deep Gray Mist	L	83
Verde Green	M	57
Burgundy Mist	N	67
Silver Mist	P	69
Signal Red	R	52
Champagne Mist	S	63
Olive Beige	T	82
Sunset Silver	V	81
Copper Mist	W	85
Cameo Cream	Y	40
Antique Gold	Z	77

Service Department
BUICK MOTOR DIVISION
Flint, Michigan

BUICK DEALER
SERVICE INFORMATION
BULLETIN

BUICK MOTOR DIVISION • GENERAL MOTORS CORPORATION • FLINT, MICHIGAN 48550

May 2, 1969

TO ALL BUICK DEALERS

SUBJECT: Recommendations For Heavy Duty Operation of 1969 350, 400, 430 Cu. In. Engines

If a 1969 Buick equipped with 350, 400 or 430 cu. in. engine is to be operated under heavy duty conditions (sustained high speeds, trailer towing, police use, commercial use) it is recommended that a new oil pump relief valve spring (Gr. 1.609, Part #1233892, Dealer Price $.56) be installed. This new spring will increase the pump regulating pressure from 50 psi to 60 psi at normal oil temperatures. This new relief valve spring went into production with engine code RS386 on all after job G. S. 400, Stage I equipped cars.

On vehicles operated as stated above, it is further recommended that 10W40, 20W or 30W viscosity oil be used, which are intended for service M.S. and meet G.M. Standard 6041-M. Increased oil viscosity is necessary to maintain adequate engine oil pressure during conditions of high engine oil temperatures.

Service Department
BUICK MOTOR DIVISION
Flint, Michigan

BUICK DEALER
SERVICE INFORMATION
BULLETIN

BUICK MOTOR DIVISION • GENERAL MOTORS CORPORATION • FLINT, MICHIGAN 48550

TO ALL BUICK DEALERS   June 2, 1969

SUBJECT: Limited Production Run on 1970 Overhead Valve System Installed on
1969 Engines

Approximately 2,500 350 cu.in. engines and 2,500 430 cu.in. engines have been built
during the first two weeks of May with the 1970 overhead valve system installed.
All of these 430 cu.in. engines will be installed in Rivieras. The 1970 overhead
replacement parts, see illustration, are released through the Parts Department and
are available at this time.

This bulletin supplies such information as: engine identification, operation, part
numbers for replacement parts, service procedures, return of parts and RO/AFA and
flat rate information.

ENGINE IDENTIFICATION

All 350 and 430 cu.in. engines with the 1970 overhead system installed will have a
modified engine date code number. The "R" in the code number designating 1969 will
be dropped from the code date. The engine designation letters D, O, and P will become the first letter. The second letter will be the designation for the 1970
overhead. The letter "X" will be used on the 350 cu.in. engine and "Y" on the 430
cu.in. engines. The three digits of the day code will not be disturbed. Following
are examples of the present engine date code number and the one used for the 1970
overhead.

                 350 Cu. In. Engine With 2-Barrel Carburetor

```
R O  123                              O X  123
  |   └── Production Day Built          |   └── Production Day Built
  └──── Engine (2bbl 350)               └───── Engine With 1970 Overhead
  └── Year                              └───── Engine (2bbl 350)

PRESENT IDENTIFICATION                ENGINE WITH 1970 OVERHEAD
```

                 350 Cu. In. Engine With 4-Barrel Carburetor

```
R P  123                              P X  123
  |   └── Production Day Built          |   └── Production Day Built
  └──── Engine (4bbl 350)               └───── Engine With 1970 Overhead
  └── Year                              └───── Engine (4bbl 350)

PRESENT IDENTIFICATION                ENGINE WITH 1970 OVERHEAD
```

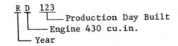

R D 123
       └── Production Day Built
       └── Engine 430 cu.in.
   └── Year

PRESENT IDENTIFICATION

D Y 123
       └── Production Day Built
       └── Engine with 1970 Overhead
   └── Engine (430 cu.in)

ENGINE WITH 1970 OVERHEAD

OPERATION

The 1970 engine overhead valve system differs from the 1969 in that oil is supplied to each rocker arm via a hole in the lifter push rod seat and a hollow push rod.

To incorporate this new design overhead system in the 1969 engine, the normal oil feed hole in the cylinder block had to be plugged to prevent oil flow through the rocker arm shaft.

The oil feed line in the cylinder block is plugged with a lead ball, which is driven flush with the top of the bank face. Under no circumstances should this plug be removed as oil hemorrhaging will result which could cause a loss of oil pressure and affect the complete engine.

PART NUMBERS

See illustration.

SERVICE PROCEDURES

Removal and installation of the 1970 overhead system remains basically the same as 1969. However, to remove and install the rocker arm retainers, proceed as follows:

1. Remove rocker arm retainer with pliers and _discard_. Do Not reuse old retainer.

2. Install _new_ rocker arm retainer, Gr. 0.349, Part #1234424, using a 3/8" diameter _flat_ punch or drift. Care should be used to ensure that retainer is driven in straight and retainer head is seated against rocker arm shaft.

RETURN OF PARTS

It is important that any replaced part be properly tagged and shipped Parcel Post to the following address as soon as possible.

> BUICK MOTOR DIVISION
> General Motors Corporation
> Clear Signal Area - Factory #2
> Flint, Michigan 48550
>
> Attn: G. A. Rolleston

RO/AFA AND FLAT RATE INFORMATION

An RO/AFA should be submitted in the normal manner keeping in mind that the current Flat Rate Operations and Rates are applicable to this new overhead system.

The claim code best describing the part which caused the failure should be used.

> Service Department
> BUICK MOTOR DIVISION
> Flint, Michigan

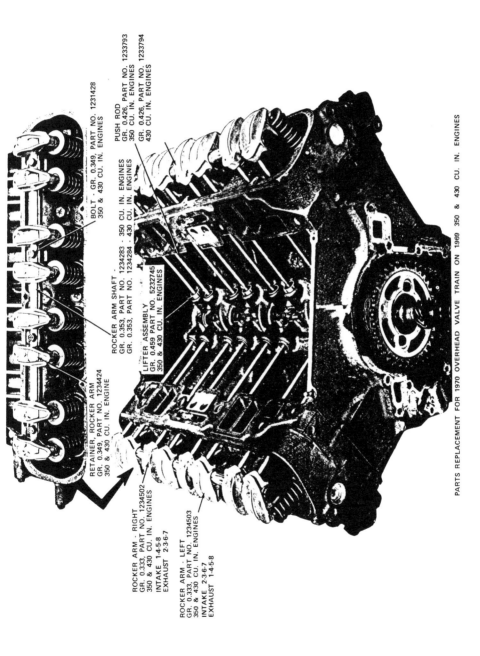

BOLT - GR. 0.349, PART NO. 1231428
350 & 430 CU. IN. ENGINES

PUSH ROD -
GR. 0.426, PART NO. 1233793
350 CU. IN. ENGINES
GR. 0.426, PART NO. 1233794
430 CU. IN. ENGINES

ROCKER ARM SHAFT -
GR. 0.353, PART NO. 1234283 - 350 CU. IN. ENGINES
GR. 0.353, PART NO. 1234284 - 430 CU. IN. ENGINES

LIFTER ASSEMBLY -
GR. 0.459 PART NO. 5232745
350 & 430 CU. IN. ENGINES

RETAINER, ROCKER ARM -
GR. 0.349, PART NO. 1234424
350 & 430 CU. IN. ENGINE

ROCKER ARM - RIGHT
GR. 0.333, PART NO. 1234502
350 & 430 CU. IN. ENGINES
INTAKE 1-4-5-8
EXHAUST 2-3-6-7

ROCKER ARM - LEFT
GR. 0.333, PART NO. 1234503
350 & 430 CU. IN. ENGINES
INTAKE 2-3-6-7
EXHAUST 1-4-5-8

PARTS REPLACEMENT FOR 1970 OVERHEAD VALVE TRAIN ON 1969 350 & 430 CU. IN. ENGINES

133

BUICK DEALER
SERVICE INFORMATION
BULLETIN

BUICK MOTOR DIVISION • **GENERAL MOTORS CORPORATION** • **FLINT, MICHIGAN 48550**

November 1, 1968

TO ALL BUICK DEALERS

SUBJECT: 1969 Buick 400 and 430 Engines Assembled With 1968 Cylinder Heads

Two hundred 1969 400 and 430 cu.in. engines were assembled with 1968 cylinder heads. These are identified with Engine Code Numbers 003 and 004. Thus if work is performed on these particular engines, 1968 exhaust valves must be installed if replacements are needed since 1968 and 1969 exhaust valves are not interchangeable.

Parts identification to distinguish 1968 from 1969 cylinder heads:

1968	1969
Both intake and exhaust valve guides are same height.	Exhaust valve guides are longer than intake valve guides.
Seals are used on both the intake and exhaust valve guides.	Only the intake valve guides have a seal.
Stem of exhaust valve is not under-cut. (See illustration).	Stem of exhaust valve is under-cut below spring-cap key area. (See illustration.)

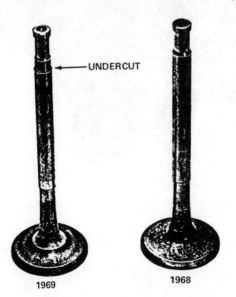

←———UNDERCUT

1969   1968

Service Department
BUICK MOTOR DIVISION
Flint, Michigan

134

BUICK DEALER
SERVICE TECHNICAL
BULLETIN

BUICK MOTOR DIVISION • GENERAL MOTORS CORPORATION • FLINT, MICHIGAN 48550

TO ALL BUICK DEALERS   February 21, 1969

SUBJECT: Whistling Noise at Intake Manifold - 1969 400 and 430 Cu. In. Engines

CONDITION

Whistling noise at intake manifold on 1969 400 and 430 cu. in. engines. Noise is present during periods of high vacuum and not present during periods of low vacuum.

CAUSE

Vacuum leak around intake ports of intake manifold.

CORRECTION

1. Remove intake manifold, gasket and end seals. Discard gasket and end seals.

2. Apply a small bead of Silastic Rubber, Gr. 8.800, Part #1051042, Dealer Price $3.00, completely around outside edge of intake ports on new gasket, Gr. 3.270, Part #1376070, Dealer Price $2.43. Repeat operation on opposite side of gasket. See Figure 1.

3. Install new intake manifold end seals, Gr. 3.270, Part #1230501, Dealer Price, $.25.

    NOTE: Before installing intake manifold side seals, apply Silastic Rubber to ends of seals. See Figure 2.

4. Install gasket and intake manifold and torque attaching bolts to 55 lb. ft. in sequence shown in Figure 3.

RO/AFA INFORMATION

When submitting RO/AFA, show Bulletin number 69-T-17 in Dealer Comment" section of this form.

Use operation number 063-525 and appropriate operation time, plus .1 hr. for application of Silastic Rubber. Use Claim Code 31 when this work is performed. Place "X" in the "P" column of the form. An amount of $.35 will be allowed for the Silastic Rubber and should be shown in the "net item" column. This information applies to this bulletin only.

                                    Service Department
                                    BUICK MOTOR DIVISION
                                    Flint, Michigan

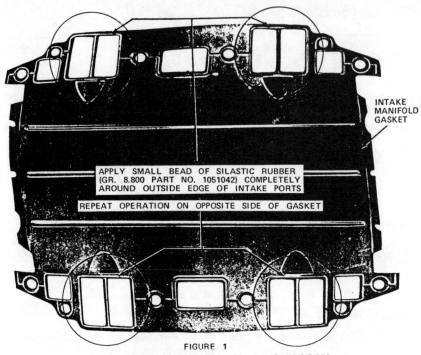

INTAKE
MANIFOLD
GASKET

APPLY SMALL BEAD OF SILASTIC RUBBER
(GR. 8.800 PART NO. 1051042) COMPLETELY
AROUND OUTSIDE EDGE OF INTAKE PORTS

REPEAT OPERATION ON OPPOSITE SIDE OF GASKET

FIGURE 1
APPLYING SILASTIC RUBBER AROUND INTAKE PORTS

APPLY SEALER TO
ENDS OF SEAL ONLY

SEAL

FIGURE 2
INTAKE MANIFOLD SIDE SEAL INSTALLATION

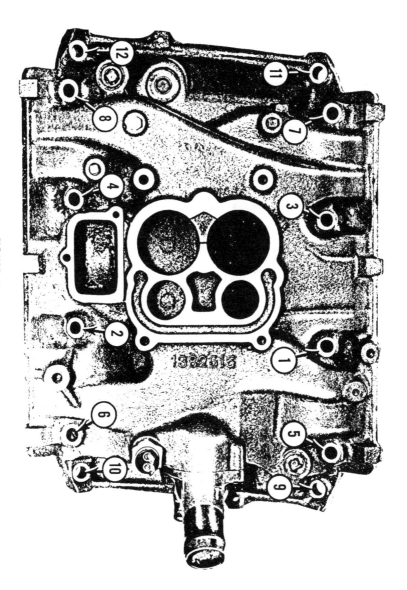

FIGURE 3
TORQUING SEQUENCE FOR INTAKE MANIFOLD ATTACHING BOLTS

BUICK DEALER
SERVICE TECHNICAL
BULLETIN

BUICK MOTOR DIVISION • GENERAL MOTORS CORPORATION • FLINT, MICHIGAN 48550

October 3, 1968

TO ALL BUICK DEALERS

SUBJECT: 1969, 430 Cubic-inch Engine Cylinder Head Metal Temperature Switch

As you know, 1969 upper-series vehicles equipped with the 430 cubic-inch engine have two (2) temperature sensing devices to provide the owner warning if the engine should overheat.

The water temperature switch is connected to the instrument panel "hot" light indicator. This light glows, showing the word "hot", when the engine coolant temperature is abnormally high.

The second device is a metal temperature sensing unit which is installed at the rear of the left cylinder head. It is connected to the instrument panel flashing light which registers "stop engine" when the temperature of the cylinder head becomes excessively hot.

It has come to our attention that the calibration of the cylinder head metal temperature switch may be incorrect on some early 1969 models, allowing the flashing "stop engine" light to come on even though the engine temperature is normal.

Steps are being taken to assure correct switch calibration and in the near future, a Service Bulletin will be issued announcing the availability of replacement switches with group and part numbers. If a vehicle is encountered with this condition, please determine if only the flashing "stop engine" light came on. If the flashing "stop engine" light came on, make sure cooling system is filled with coolant. If cooling system is satisfactory, this indicates that the switch is defective instead of an overheating condition. In these cases, disconnect wire from the switch at rear of left cylinder head and tape terminal end to prevent possible grounding; then tape wire to wiring harness on dash to prevent possible interference with other engine components. Record the owner's name and address so that a correctly calibrated switch may be installed at a later date.

The owner will still have adequate warning by the "hot" temperature light which is triggered by the water temperature switch. This is equivalent protection to the 1968 model. Of course, if both the "stop engine" light and "hot" light come on, then there is possibility that something is definitely wrong with the cooling system. In this case, the first step would be to make certain that the cooling system is properly filled. We have reports where indications were that the engine was overheating when the problem was actually due to low coolant level.

We urge all dealers to emphasize the importance of making certain that the cooling system is properly filled during the New Vehicle Pre-delivery Service and Adjustment Procedures.

Service Department
BUICK MOTOR DIVISION

INFORMATION BULLETIN NUMBER		DEALER FILE	
		Model Year	1969
69-I-21		File in Group	64
		Number	1

BUICK DEALER
SERVICE INFORMATION
BULLETIN

BUICK MOTOR DIVISION • GENERAL MOTORS CORPORATION • FLINT, MICHIGAN 48550

November 1, 1968

TO ALL BUICK DEALERS

SUBJECT: Incorrect Removal of 1969 Riviera Electric Fuel Pump

It has come to our attention that electric fuel pump-fuel gage tank unit assemblies are being damaged during removal because technicians are disconnecting the wires at the unit. This is a permanent connection - <u>disconnecting here destroys the unit</u>. See illustration.

The proper way to remove the fuel pump follows:

1. Raise car. Disconnect two-terminal connector forward of fuel tank. Remove ground wire screw.

2. Lower car. Pull back trunk floor carpeting. Remove five screws from access hole cover and remove cover.

3. Disconnect fuel hose from tank unit.

4. Unscrew retaining cam ring using Wrench J-21518 and remove fuel pump-tank unit assembly.

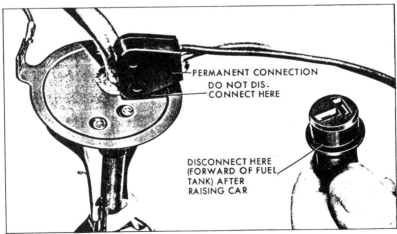

Service Department
BUICK MOTOR DIVISION
Flint, Michigan

BUICK DEALER
SERVICE TECHNICAL
BULLETIN

BUICK MOTOR DIVISION • GENERAL MOTORS CORPORATION • FLINT, MICHIGAN 48550

December 20, 1968

TO ALL BUICK DEALERS

SUBJECT: Kinked Rubber Fuel Hose - 1969 All Series

CONDITION:

Engine surge and fuel starvation at highway speeds or unable to
start - 1969 All Series.

CAUSE:

Kinked rubber gasoline hose in area of fuel tank or in area of
fuel pump.

CORRECTION:

Check rubber gasoline hose for being kinked and correct as required.

This Bulletin is for Information Only.

Service Department
BUICK MOTOR DIVISION
Flint, Michigan

BUICK DEALER
SERVICE INFORMATION
BULLETIN

BUICK MOTOR DIVISION • GENERAL MOTORS CORPORATION • FLINT, MICHIGAN 48550

TO ALL BUICK DEALERS   January 17, 1969

SUBJECT: 1969 Riviera Electric Fuel Pump Diagnosis

To supplement the 1969 Riviera electric fuel pump diagnosis information on Page 64-21 of the 1969 Chassis Service Manual, the following information is being presented.

DEAD PUMPS

Check "Gages" fuse located in the fuse block. See Figure 1. Check in-line fuse located in the in-line fuse holder in the dark blue wire at front of cowl just above brake master cylinder. See Figure 1. Care must be taken to separate fuse holder by a straight pull, not wiggling connector. Wiggling can cause fuse holder or fuse breakage.

IN-LINE FUSE CONTINUES TO BLOW REPEATEDLY

Disconnect the multiple connector, under car, from the pump-tank unit. If fuse in-line blows, the problem is pinched wire someplace in the body. See Figure 1. Use a 4-ampere, 5/8" replacement fuse Gr. 8.965, Part #147682, Dealer Price .05. If fuse does not blow, the problem is likely to be a piece of solder laying across the pump terminals. Remove tank unit and correct. Do not replace the entire tank unit assembly when a pump is found defective. Replace pump and filter unit only. Gr. 3900, Part #6417483, Dealer Price $17.69.

CAUTION: When removing tank unit, DO NOT ATTEMPT to disconnect the wires from the unit. This is a permanent connection - disconnecting here destroys the unit. See Figure 2. Always disconnect the two-terminal connector forward of the fuel tank.

NO FLOW OR INTERMITTENT FLOW

Rubber elbow between fuel pick-up tube and pump could have a loose piece of rubber flash inside. Remove elbow and inspect carefully. See Figure 3.

DEAD OR INTERMITTENT PUMP

The plastic connector which is installed on the oil pressure switch could have excess plastic on surface of terminals. If terminals are not free of plastic, clean with sharp knife. This type of condition could show up as a temperature related problem - pump runs satisfactorily when cold but cuts out when underhood temperatures are high.

PUMP WILL NOT PUMP WHEN NEW ONE IS INSTALLED, BUT PUMP RUNS

Wires to pump were reversed and pump is running backwards. The black round wire (ground) should be attached to the pump terminal closest to the tank unit float.

Service Department
BUICK MOTOR DIVISION
Flint, Michigan

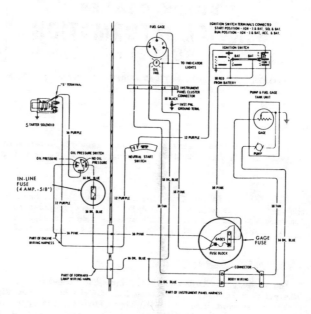

FIGURE 1

ELECTRIC FUEL PUMP CIRCUIT DIAGRAM

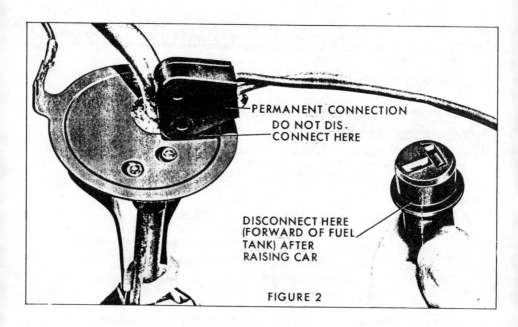

PERMANENT CONNECTION
DO NOT DIS-
CONNECT HERE

DISCONNECT HERE
(FORWARD OF FUEL
TANK) AFTER
RAISING CAR

FIGURE 2

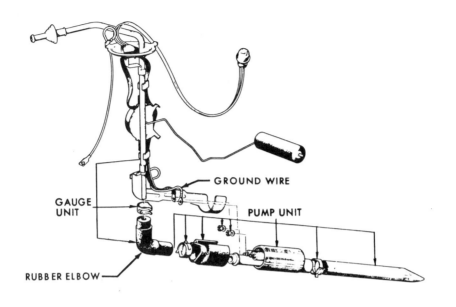

GROUND WIRE

GAUGE
UNIT

PUMP UNIT

RUBBER ELBOW

ELECTRIC FUEL PUMP AND FUEL GAGE TANK UNIT ASSEMBLY

FIGURE 3

INFORMATION BULLETIN NUMBER		DEALER FILE	
		Model Year	1969
69-I-49		File in Group	130
		Number	1

BUICK DEALER
SERVICE INFORMATION
BULLETIN

BUICK MOTOR DIVISION • GENERAL MOTORS CORPORATION • FLINT, MICHIGAN 48550

January 17, 1969

TO ALL BUICK DEALERS

SUBJECT: Release of New Radiator Pressure Cap - All
1969 Models

Starting approximately January 2, 1969, production began
using a new design radiator pressure cap and a revised
radiator filler neck on all 1969 model cars. The new
design provides a more positive stop at the pressure relief position of the cap. To remove cap from the pressure
relief position, it must be pushed down while simultaneously rotating counterclockwise.

Both the first and second designs are interchangeable.

CAUTION: To avoid loss of coolant, always check
level when engine is cold.

Service Department
BUICK MOTOR DIVISION
Flint, Michigan

BUICK DEALER
SERVICE INFORMATION
BULLETIN

BUICK MOTOR DIVISION • **GENERAL MOTORS CORPORATION** • **FLINT, MICHIGAN 48550**

October 25, 1968

<u>IMPORTANT</u>   <u>IMPORTANT</u>   <u>IMPORTANT</u>

TO ALL BUICK DEALERS

SUBJECT: RADIATOR COOLANT LEVEL - All 1969 Series Cars

It is of the utmost importance that the radiator coolant be checked and brought to the proper level, if necessary, on all 1969 Series cars, during the 1969 New Car Pre-Delivery Service. <u>If the coolant level is not accurately checked and adjustment made, when required, overheating complaints will result.</u> In order to obtain the most accurate check on coolant level, the recommended procedure outlined below must be followed.

1. With engine cold, check coolant level in radiator; if low, recommended coolant must be added to bring level to just below top of filler neck. With radiator cap removed, start engine and run at fast idle until upper radiator inlet hose is <u>HOT</u>. (Hot hose will indicate that the engine thermostat is open).

   IMPORTANT: <u>On all Air Conditioner Equipped Cars, Make Certain the Water Temperature Control Valve is Open.</u> To open the valve, move the heater temperature control to <u>MAXIMUM</u> temperature position and check for vacuum applied to water valve diaphragm.

   NOTE: Alcohol or methanol base coolants or plain water are not recommended for the cooling system at any time. Use only ethylene glycol type anti-corrosive anti-freeze and protect to a minimum of -20°F.

2. At first opportunity, after car has been driven under normal operating conditions, with the heater temperature control placed in maximum temperature position, the coolant level should again be checked with the engine <u>COLD</u>. If low, add recommended coolant to bring level just below filler neck.

3. In extreme cases, air may still be trapped in the cooling system. To purge the system of air, run the engine at speeds of 1500-2000 RPM, with thermostat wide open, for a period of time after the upper radiator hose has become hot as described in step #1. This will insure that all air is displaced with coolant.

   NOTE: Trapped air in the cooling system in some cases is very difficult to recognize because the system will appear full until operated as described above.

   IMPORTANT: <u>Do not attempt any corrective work on engine such as changing thermostats, water pumps or hoses until the above items have been checked and adjusted.</u>

Service Department
BUICK MOTOR DIVISION
Flint, Michigan

⊛

BUICK DEALER
SERVICE INFORMATION
BULLETIN

BUICK MOTOR DIVISION • GENERAL MOTORS CORPORATION • FLINT, MICHIGAN 48550

May 2, 1969

TO ALL BUICK DEALERS

SUBJECT: Telltail Odometer - All 1969 Models Built After
January 1, 1969

All 1969 Buicks built after January 1, 1969, have a telltail
odometer. This odometer provides <u>VISUAL</u> evidence if a forcible
attempt has been made to reset mileage.

IMPORTANT: THE BUICK NEW VEHICLE WARRANTY SHALL NOT APPLY
TO ANY VEHICLE ON WHICH THE ODOMETER MILEAGE
HAS BEEN ALTERED AND THE VEHICLE'S ACTUAL
MILEAGE CANNOT BE READILY DETERMINED.

If the first or second figure wheel and/or pinion carriers have
been forcibly rotated in an attempt to change the odometer mileage
reading, a white portion of these pinion carriers is exposed instead of the normal black color. See illustration. The color
change occurs due to the fact that forcing the odometer wheels or
pinion carriers will break a plastic "carrier breakaway strip"
which holds the carriers in alignment. Breaking of the strip allows
the first and second carriers to rotate, thus, exposing the white
surface color.

Service Department
BUICK MOTOR DIVISION
Flint, Michigan

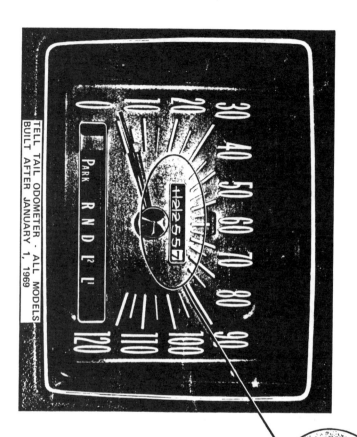

TELL TAIL ODOMETER - ALL MODELS BUILT AFTER JANUARY 1, 1969

WHITE PORTION OF PINION CARRIERS ARE EXPOSED WHEN A FORCIBLE ATTEMPT IS MADE TO CHANGE THE ODOMETER READING.

INFORMATION BULLETIN NUMBER
69-I-64

(W)

BUICK DEALER
SERVICE INFORMATION
BULLETIN

DEALER FILE	
Model Year	1969
File in Group	120
Number	5

BUICK MOTOR DIVISION • GENERAL MOTORS CORPORATION • FLINT, MICHIGAN 48550

March 7, 1969

TO ALL BUICK DEALERS

SUBJECT: Anti-Reversing Odometers - All 1969 Models

Beginning with 1969 production, all speedometers are equipped with an anti-reversing odometer.

Anti-reverse involves a special cam and gear assembly between the odometer drive wheel and decimal wheel which restricts odometer operation to only the forward direction. If the odometer is driven in a reverse direction, as with an attempted mileage reduction, the mating cam and gear become disengaged and the odometer ceases operation.

NOTE: If a vehicle equipped with the anti-reverse odometer is driven in reverse, immediate disengagement occurs. If the distance (reverse) is less than 1/4 mile, odometer re-engagement will occur when the vehicle is driven a duplicate distance forward. If the distance (reverse) is more than 1/4 mile, re-engagement will normally occur within one mile. Occasionally, however, the vehicle will have to be driven in the forward direction for up to 5 miles before re-engagement occurs. If at this time, re-engagement does not occur, the odometer may be considered defective.

In some cases these speedometers have been removed for repair unnecessarily due to inoperative odometers. These odometers should not be considered non-functional until the cars have been operated in a forward direction for a minimum of five miles.

Service Department
BUICK MOTOR DIVISION
Flint, Michigan

BUICK DEALER
SERVICE TECHNICAL
BULLETIN

BUICK MOTOR DIVISION • GENERAL MOTORS CORPORATION • FLINT, MICHIGAN 48550

TO ALL BUICK DEALERS   February 21, 1969

SUBJECT: Turbo Hydra-Matic 400 Transmission Oil Filter Assembly - All Present and Past Models

PROBLEM

Complaints such as "transmission noisy", "noisy pump", "sounds like a siren", "slips", "no upshift", "no drive" and "temporary loss of drive after a stop".

CAUSE

In many cases these types of complaints are due to a plugged or restricted transmission oil filter, incorrect filter usage, split intake pipe or defective intake pipe or defective intake pipe "O" ring.

MODELS AFFECTED

All present and past model Turbo Hydra-Matic 400 Transmissions.

CORRECTION

If a complaint is encountered such as described above, the information below concerning transmission oil filters should be noted.

1. The filter assembly should be replaced on transmissions overhauled for any major failure where clutch plate material or excessive metal particles are found in the pan.

   1969, 1968 and late 1967 filters are a full flow design and do not have a by-pass valve. When this filter becomes contaminated, it will restrict the intake to the transmission pump and will result in one or more of the above malfunctions.

2. There are two designs of the filter assembly, and they are not interchangeable. First design filters were used on 1964, 1965, 1966 and early 1967 transmissions. See Figure 1, View A. Second design filters were used in 1969, 1968 and late 1967 transmissions. See Figure 1, View B. Transmission failure will result from an incorrect combination of oil pan and filter.

   The first type pan (See Figure 1, View A) is not deep enough to accommodate the flat second type filter assembly (See Figure 1, View B) and if their installation as a combination is attempted, the filter assembly will be crushed.

   When service replacement of the filter assembly and/or oil pan is required, they must be used in the combinations illustrated in Figure 1.

3. The intake pipe must be checked to make certain it is not split or otherwise defective.

Service Department
BUICK MOTOR DIVISION
Flint, Michigan

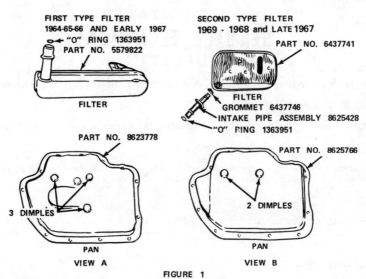

FIRST TYPE FILTER
1964-65-66 AND EARLY 1967
"O" RING 1363951
PART NO. 5579822

FILTER

SECOND TYPE FILTER
1969 - 1968 and LATE 1967

PART NO. 6437741

FILTER
GROMMET 6437746
INTAKE PIPE ASSEMBLY 8625428
"O" RING 1363951

PART NO. 8623778

3 DIMPLES

PAN

VIEW A

PART NO. 8625766

2 DIMPLES

PAN

VIEW B

FIGURE 1
FIRST & SECOND TYPE TURBO HYDRA-MATIC 400 FILTERS AND OIL PANS

BUICK DEALER SERVICE INFORMATION BULLETIN

BUICK MOTOR DIVISION • GENERAL MOTORS CORPORATION • FLINT, MICHIGAN 48550

February 14, 1969

TO ALL BUICK DEALERS

SUBJECT: 1964 - 1969 Turbo Hydra-Matic 400 Case Extension to Case Paper Gasket

The 1964-65-66 Turbo Hydra-matic 400 transmission case extension face had a machined groove and used a square cut seal ring to seal between the transmission case and case extension. See Figure 1.

In 1967, the machined groove was eliminated in the face of the case extension and a paper gasket was used to seal between the transmission case and case extension. See Figure 2. The paper gasket is also used for 1968 and 1969 transmissions.

The square cut seal ring has been cancelled. Either type case extension may be used for Service and the paper gasket, Gr. 4.318, Part #8624709, Dealer Price $.13, should be used with both case extensions.

Service Department
BUICK MOTOR DIVISION
Flint, Michigan

151

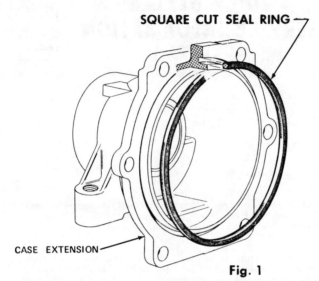

SQUARE CUT SEAL RING

CASE EXTENSION

Fig. 1

1964-1965-1966 CASE EXTENSION AND SQUARE CUT SEAL RING

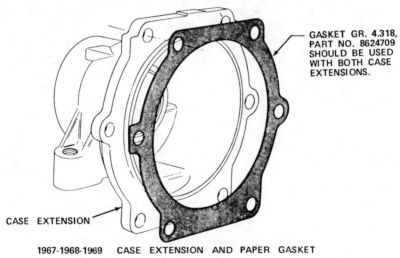

GASKET GR. 4.318,
PART NO. 8624709
SHOULD BE USED
WITH BOTH CASE
EXTENSIONS.

CASE EXTENSION

1967-1968-1969 CASE EXTENSION AND PAPER GASKET

Fig. 2

BUICK DEALER
SERVICE INFORMATION
BULLETIN

BUICK MOTOR DIVISION • GENERAL MOTORS CORPORATION • FLINT, MICHIGAN 48550

October 25, 1968

TO ALL BUICK DEALERS

SUBJECT: Cruise Master Transducer Usage

The 1968 and 1969 Cruise Master transducers externally appear to be identical, but internally are different. <u>These two units are not interchangeable</u>. Transducers are released through the Parts Department as follows:

1968			1969		
Group	Part No.	Model	Group	Part No.	Model
3.885	6465434	43-44-45-46-48000	3.885	6465584	43-44-45-46-48-49000
3.885	6465435	49000			

Service Department
BUICK MOTOR DIVISION
Flint, Michigan

CHAPTER SEVEN

1970 RIVIERA

INFORMATION BULLETIN NUMBER
70-I-41

BUICK DEALER
SERVICE INFORMATION
BULLETIN

DEALER FILE	
Model Year	**1970**
File in Group	60
Number	2

BUICK MOTOR DIVISION • GENERAL MOTORS CORPORATION • FLINT, MICHIGAN 48550

February 6, 1970

TO ALL BUICK DEALERS

SUBJECT: Puff of Smoke on Immediate Start-Up - 1970 455 Cubic Inch Engines

The puff of smoke, which is a normal condition, is the result of the new valve train system and the greater quantity of oil flowing in the overhead area. The 350 cubic inch engine, with valve stem seals on all valves, will not exhibit this condition. The 455 cubic inch engine does not have valve seals on the exhaust, instead, the valve stem incorporates a scraper that pushes the oil up the stem not allowing excessive oil to enter the combustion chamber.

When the engine is shut off, the slight amount of oil remaining on the valve stem will drain down the stem and into the combustion chamber. When the engine is again started, the small puff of smoke will be evident, which as stated above is a normal condition.

Tests have shown that the smoking condition has no effect on oil consumption.

Service Department
BUICK MOTOR DIVISION
Flint, Michigan

BUICK DEALER
SERVICE INFORMATION
BULLETIN

BUICK MOTOR DIVISION • GENERAL MOTORS CORPORATION • FLINT, MICHIGAN 48550

TO ALL BUICK DEALERS   March 6, 1970

SUBJECT: Engine Start Up Connecting Rod Main Bearing Knock Diagnosis - All
          Present and Past Models

CONDITION

Engine start up connecting rod or main bearing knock - All present and past models.

CAUSE

1. Excessive vertical clearance caused by loose bearing fit or insufficient
   clearance for proper lubrication.

2. Misassembly of rod and cap (wrong or reversed cap).

3. Lack of lubrication.

DIAGNOSIS

A. Rod Bearing Knock

   Rod bearing knock is a light and _rapid_ sounding knock which occurs when the
   engine is cold and rapidly diminishes and disappears when oil pressure builds
   up. It is often referred to as a "machine gun type" rattle that is gone by
   the time the engine oil light goes off. This type of knock normally occurs
   when the vertical clearance exceeds .0025".

B. Rod Bearing Knock Related To Rod and Cap Misassembly

   Knocks related to rod and cap misassembly are distinguished by the fact
   that they can occur with cold and/or hot engines. The sound of the knock
   is usually more distinct and heavier, similiar to a main bearing knock.

C. Main Bearing Knock

   Main bearing knock is a heavy sounding knock more solid than a rod knock.
   It will usually diminish and disappear as oil pressure builds up.

D. Lubrication Oriented Knocks

   Lubrication oriented knocks are extremely difficult to diagnose because
   the clearances are normally acceptable and no assembly problems are found.
   Investigation usually reveals:

   1. Suction leak due to a loose or split oil pump pickup tube. This will

cause aeration of the oil.

2. Restriction of the oil pump inlet due to a mislocated oil pump cover gasket.

3. Low oil pressure due to pump pressure relief valve stuck open by foreign material.

CORRECTION

Rod Bearings and Main Bearing Knocks

1. Check rod cap bolt torque.

2. Check all rods and mains for fit by removing cap and plastigaging with original bearings as described in the Buick Chassis Service Manual.

3. A knock related to rod and cap misassembly (See item B, under Diagnosis) must first have cap bolt torque checked. If bolt torque is within specification, remove cap and examine the wear pattern on the cap bearing insert. Cap misassembly will result in an unequal wear pattern on the bearing inserts.

   To establish if the wrong cap was installed, remove the rod assembly from the engine. Then, reassemble the rod and cap without bearing inserts. Look for misalignment at the split line between rod and cap, (Both bearing bore and outside surface), (See Figure 1, View A) resulting in an unequal width of I.D. chamfer at the split line. (See Figure 1, View B). If the rod and cap are correctly assembled, the side face grinder highlights will carry through the split line with perfect alignment. See Figure 1, View C.

   NOTE: It sometimes requires the use of a magnifying glass to see the grinder marks.

   Cap misassembly is often reported as "out-of-round" rod bores. In all reported cases, it has been misassembly of the rod cap. It is important to note that some misalignment can occur at the split line due to tolerances, however, the chamfer width and grinder mark alignment will always hold true on the correct cap. See Figure 1, View C. When checking a rod for being out-of-round, measure in areas indicated in Figure 2.

   To eliminate cap misassembly in production, a paint identification system is now in use. This system consists of diagonal lines of paint or a paint daub (See Figure 3) across the mating surface of the connecting rod and cap. This marking will only be retained on low mileage vehicles as the identification marks are lost after engine operation.

Service Department
BUICK MOTOR DIVISION
Flint, Michigan

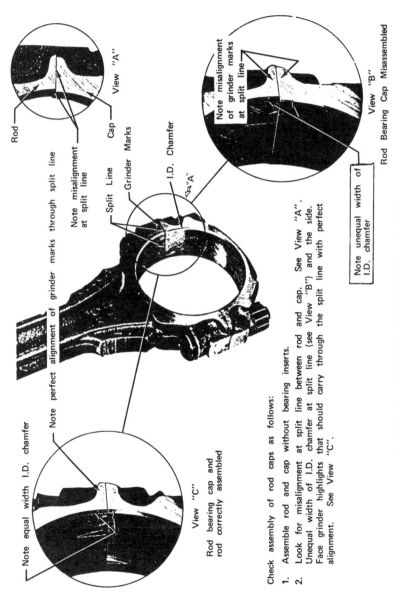

Rod

Note misalignment
at split line

View "A"

Cap

Note perfect alignment of grinder marks through split line

Split Line

Grinder Marks

I.D. Chamfer

Note misalignment
of grinder marks
at split line

View "A"

View "B"

Rod Bearing Cap Misassembled

Note unequal width of
I.D. chamfer

Note equal width I.D. chamfer

View "C"

Rod bearing cap and
rod correctly assembled

Check assembly of rod caps as follows:

1. Assemble rod and cap without bearing inserts.

2. Look for misalignment at split line between rod and cap. See View "A".
    Unequal width of I.D. chamfer at split line (see View "B") and the side.
    Face grinder highlights that should carry through the split line with perfect
    alignment. See View "C".

FIGURE 1 - CHECKING ASSEMBLY OF BEARING CAP

159

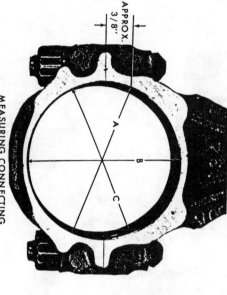

APPROX.
3/8"

A
B
C

MEASURING CONNECTING
ROD FOR "OUT-OF-ROUND".
DIMENSION "A", "B" AND "C" SHOULD
BE THE SAME WITHIN .0005" IN.

FIGURE 2
CHECKING ROD FOR BEING OUT-OF-ROUND

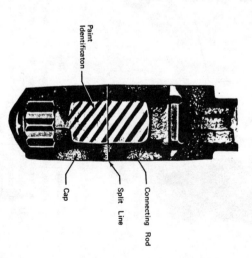

Paint
Identificaton

Cap

Split Line

Connecting Rod

FIGURE 3 - Production Paint Identification on Rod & Cup

INFORMATION BULLETIN NUMBER		DEALER FILE	
	BUICK DEALER	Model Year	1970
	SERVICE INFORMATION	File in Group	60
70-I-80			
	BULLETIN	Number	9

BUICK MOTOR DIVISION • GENERAL MOTORS CORPORATION • FLINT, MICHIGAN 48550

May 1, 1970

TO ALL BUICK DEALERS

SUBJECT: Presence of Oil in Radiator and Surge Tank

With reference to Service Information Bulletin 70-T-11, File Group 60-4, Dated February 20, 1970, we would again like to point out that a stop leak material is being used in production as an added prevention for cylinder head gasket leaks.

WHEN STOP LEAK MATERIAL IS ADDED TO THE COOLING SYSTEM, IN SERVICE, THE PRESENCE OF OIL WILL BE FOUND IN THE SURGE TANK AS WELL AS THE RADIATOR, DUE TO THE STOP LEAK MATERIAL HAVING AN OIL SOLUBLE BASE. THIS IS NORMAL.

Therefore, for this reason, the presence of oil in the cooling system does not necessarily mean that a head gasket has failed. Engine or transmission oil in the cooling system will be quite evident in that the amount of oil in the radiator and surge tank will vary considerably from the amount of oil deposited from the stop leak material. The soluble oil in the stop leak material will accumulate to a depth of 1/8 to 1/4 inch whereas engine or transmission oil will generally be 3 to 5 inches in depth depending on the severity of the leak and length of time the vehicle has been driven. Also a loss of oil in these components will generally be noted.

Service Department
BUICK MOTOR DIVISION
Flint, Michigan

INFORMATION BULLETIN NUMBER		DEALER FILE	
70-I-78	BUICK DEALER **SERVICE INFORMATION** BULLETIN	Model Year	1970
		File in Group	60
		Number	7

BUICK MOTOR DIVISION • GENERAL MOTORS CORPORATION • FLINT, MICHIGAN 48550

May 1, 1970

TO ALL BUICK DEALERS

SUBJECT: Oil Gauge Rod and Oil Pan Baffle Interference

When checking the engine oil level, should the oil gauge
rod become even slightly bent it should be straightened.

A slightly bent oil gauge rod thrust into the gauging
hole in the engine block may miss the hole in the oil pan
baffle inside the crankcase. Instead of passing through the
oil pan baffle and into the oil, the oil gauge rod will bend
around the oil pan baffle. This can produce erroneous oil
level readings and may cause an interference between the oil
gauge rod and the crankshaft, with resultant engine damage.

Service Department
BUICK MOTOR DIVISION
Flint, Michigan

INFORMATION BULLETIN NUMBER		DEALER FILE	
	BUICK DEALER	Model Year	1970
70-I-92	SERVICE INFORMATION	File in Group	74
	BULLETIN	Number	20

BUICK MOTOR DIVISION • **GENERAL MOTORS CORPORATION** • **FLINT, MICHIGAN 48550**

May 22, 1970

TO ALL BUICK DEALERS

SUBJECT: Production Trial Run With Intake Pipe Assembly Made of Plastic Instead of Steel

A production trial run has been completed, using an intake pipe assembly made of plastic instead of steel in some 1970 Turbo Hydramatic "400" Transmissions. See illustration.

The transmission serial numbers and build date codes of transmissions containing the plastic intake pipe are as follows:

TRANSMISSION SERIAL NOS.	BUILD DATE CODES
70-BC-171356 thru 70-BC-173932	458 thru 462

Service Information

The plastic intake pipe assembly and steel intake pipe assembly are completely interchangeable. However, the plastic intake pipe assembly is not available for service at this time; therefore, should replacement become necessary, use the current steel intake pipe assembly, Group #4.197, Part #8625428.

Service Department
BUICK MOTOR DIVISION
Flint, Michigan

THE TRANSMISSION SERIAL NUMBERS AND
BUILD DATE CODES OF TRANSMISSIONS
CONTAINING THE PLASTIC INTAKE PIPE
ARE AS FOLLOWS:

TRANSMISSION SER. NOS.   DATE CODES

70-BC-171356 THRU   458 THRU
70-BC-173932   462

SHOULD REPLACEMENT BECOME NECESSARY
USE CURRENT STEEL INTAKE PIPE ASSEMBLY
GROUP NO. 4.197, PART NO. 8625428.

STRAINER
ASSEMBLY

PLASTIC
INTAKE
PIPE

O-RING SEAL

LOCATOR
TABS

INTAKE PIPE ASSEMBLY
THM "400" TRANSMISSION

74.862

164

INFORMATION BULLETIN NUMBER		DEALER FILE	
		Model Year	1970
70-I-107		File in Group	74
		Number	24

BUICK DEALER
SERVICE INFORMATION
BULLETIN

BUICK MOTOR DIVISION • GENERAL MOTORS CORPORATION • FLINT, MICHIGAN 48550

July 8, 1970

TO ALL BUICK DEALERS

SUBJECT: Reemphasis Of Center Support and Intermediate Clutch Snap Ring Usage
All Turbo Hydra-matic 400 Transmissions

There are continuing reports of field failures after overhaul of the THM-400 Transmission as a result of interchanging the center support retaining snap ring with the intermediate clutch backing plate retaining snap ring.

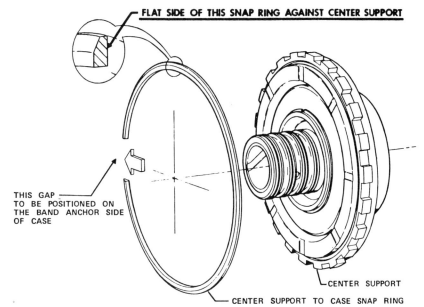

FLAT SIDE OF THIS SNAP RING AGAINST CENTER SUPPORT

THIS GAP TO BE POSITIONED ON THE BAND ANCHOR SIDE OF CASE

CENTER SUPPORT

CENTER SUPPORT TO CASE SNAP RING

THE CENTER SUPPORT TO CASE SNAP RING HAS ONE SIDE BEVELED AND ONE SIDE FLAT. THE SNAP RING GROOVE IN THE CASE HAS ONE SIDE TAPERED, TO ACCOMMODATE THE BEVELED RING. THE CENTER SUPPORT BEVELED SNAP RING SHOULD BE INSTALLED WITH THE FLAT SIDE AGAINST THE CENTER SUPPORT AND WITH THE RING GAP ADJACENT TO THE BAND ANCHOR PIN.

FIGURE 1

The intermediate clutch backing plate to case snap ring is flat on both sides and the snap ring groove in the case has straight sides to accommodate it. The beveled center support to case snap ring will not properly seat in this groove and if installed here, it will come out during operation, frequently breaking the spline in the case from the snap ring groove forward. Either one of which would result in a transmission failure.

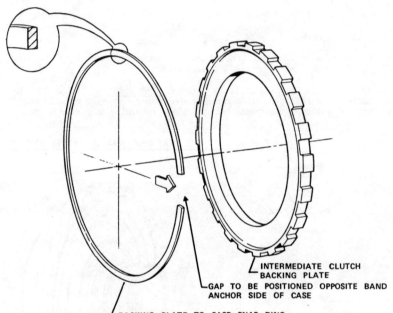

INTERMEDIATE CLUTCH BACKING PLATE
GAP TO BE POSITIONED OPPOSITE BAND ANCHOR SIDE OF CASE
BACKING PLATE TO CASE SNAP RING

INSTALL THE INTERMEDIATE CLUTCH BACKING PLATE TO CASE FLAT SNAP RING WITH THE RING GAP OPPOSITE THE BAND ANCHOR PIN.
FIGURE 2

Service Department
BUICK MOTOR DIVISION
Flint, Michigan

INFORMATION BULLETIN NUMBER		DEALER FILE	
		Model Year	1970
70-I-35		File in Group	74
		Number	9

BUICK DEALER
SERVICE INFORMATION
BULLETIN

BUICK MOTOR DIVISION • **GENERAL MOTORS CORPORATION** • **FLINT, MICHIGAN 48550**

December 29, 1969

TO ALL BUICK DEALERS

SUBJECT: Turbo Hydra-Matic 400 Transmissions - Latest Type Service Control
Valve Body Assembly Casting For Past Model Use

Service control valve assemblies for past models (except 1964) will be manufactured using the latest type body castings. In these assemblies, a pipe
plug is installed in a tapped hole in the body casting next to the front accumulator pocket (see illustration). The plug must remain securely installed.
Omission of the plug will cause the direct clutch to slip and eventually burn
during third gear and reverse operation.

NOTE: Service control valve assemblies for 1970 models are also built with
the plug installed in the body casting. When installing these assemblies into 1970 models using the pressure switch, remove plug and
securely install switch. If no pressure switch is used, the plug
must remain securely installed.

PLEASE MAKE CERTAIN THAT ALL AUTOMATIC TRANSMISSION TECHNICIANS ARE MADE
AWARE OF THE ABOVE CHANGES.

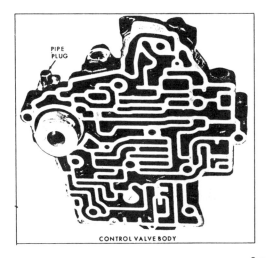

PIPE
PLUG

CONTROL VALVE BODY

Service Department
BUICK MOTOR DIVISION
Flint, Michigan

INFORMATION BULLETIN NUMBER
70-I-84

BUICK DEALER
SERVICE INFORMATION
BULLETIN

DEALER FILE	
Model Year	1970
File in Group	68
Number	5

BUICK MOTOR DIVISION • GENERAL MOTORS CORPORATION • FLINT, MICHIGAN 48550

May 8, 1970

TO ALL BUICK DEALERS

SUBJECT: Cruise Master Speed Adjustment

It has been brought to the attention of the Service Department that some Cruise Master Transducers are being removed as defective, when in reality all they need is a speed adjustment.

If the car cruises at a speed above or below the engagement speed this error can be corrected with a simple adjustment of the orifice tube in the transducer. See illustration.

CAUTION: Do not completely remove the orifice tube from the transducer.

To check cruise speed error, engage the Cruise Master at 60 MPH. If car cruises below engagement speed, screw orifice tube outward. If car cruises above engagement speed, screw orifice tube inward. Each 1/4 turn of the orifice tube will change the cruise speed approximately one MPH. Snug-up the lock nut after each adjustment before testing.

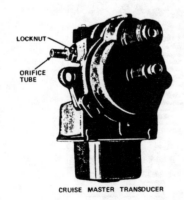

LOCKNUT

ORIFICE TUBE

CRUISE MASTER TRANSDUCER

Service Department
BUICK MOTOR DIVISION
Flint, Michigan

BUICK DEALER
SERVICE INFORMATION
BULLETIN

BUICK MOTOR DIVISION • GENERAL MOTORS CORPORATION • FLINT, MICHIGAN 48550

November 14, 1969

TO ALL BUICK DEALERS

SUBJECT: 1969 & 1970 NOISY CB RADIOS (RIVIERA ONLY)

When the Riviera electric fuel pump is running, it sometimes generates an electric impulse that falls within the citizens band radio frequency. This impulse can be identified as a high pitch growl heard through the CB radio speaker.

The following information will aid in closing an owner's complaint of a noisy CB radio.

1. Obtain a 0.5 mfd, 200 volt by-pass capacitor. (Use a good quality moisture-proof capacitor, preferably plastic encapsulated.)

2. Disconnect ground cable from battery.

3. Pull back carpet in trunk (jackside) to expose electric fuel pump access cover (see figure #1).

4. Remove access cover.

5. Carefully remove a small portion of insulation from the dark blue wire. (Do not cut wire.) Figure 2.

6. Note, if capacitor is marked positive and ground. (Not all capacitors have this identification.)

7. Insulate positive side of capacitor lead with a good electric insulating tape or use a piece of outer insulation (known as spaghetti) removed from a wire the same size as the capacitor lead.

8. Wrap the exposed end of the insulated lead around the bare section of the dark blue wire.

9. Solder the wires together. (CAUTION: DO NOT USE A FLAME OR ACID CORE SOLDER.)

10. Tape solder connection.

11. Solder ground lead of capacitor to ground lug on tank.

BUICK	
Authorized	
Service	

BUICK DEALER
SERVICE INFORMATION
BULLETIN

Model Year	1971
Bulletin No.	71-I-33A
File in Group	60
Number	1
Date	2-5-71

SUBJECT: Revision to Engine and Camshaft Identification Bulletin

MODELS AFFECTED: 1971 Models

This bulletin is being issued to provide additional camshaft identification information and supercedes Bulletin 71-I-33 dated December 11, 1970.

The following chart and illustration contain the 1971 Engine and Camshaft Identification, as well as the various models in which a particular engine or camshaft is used.

ENGINE AND CAMSHAFT IDENTIFICATION CHART

1971 Prefix	Displacement Cubic Inch	Compression Ratio-1971	Carburetor	Camshaft - 1971	Transmission Man.	Transmission Auto.	Car Series
			DOMESTIC ENGINES				
*	250 (L-6)	8.5:1	1 Bbl.		X	X	43-44000
TO	350	8.5:1	2 Bbl.	1237736	X	X	43-44000
					X		45000
TC	350	8.5 to 1	2 Bbl.	1237651		X	45000
TB	350	8.5 to 1	4 Bbl.	1237736	X		43-44000
TD	350	8.5 to 1	4 Bbl.	1237651		X	43-44-45000
TR	455	8.5 to 1	4 Bbl.	1237665		X	46-48-49000
					X	X	44000-GS
					X		46000
TS	455	8.5 to 1	4 Bbl.	1383853	X	X	44000-GS(Stage I)
TA	455	8.5 to 1	4 Bbl.	1237664		X	49000-GS
							46000 Option (Centurion Only)
			EXPORT ENGINES				
TW	350	8.0 to 1	2 Bbl.	1237736	X	X	43-44000
						X	45000

* The L-6 will carry Chevrolet's method of Identification.

Example:

Plant	Month	Day	Engine
F	12	07	ZB - Manual Transmission
			ZG - Automatic Transmission

173

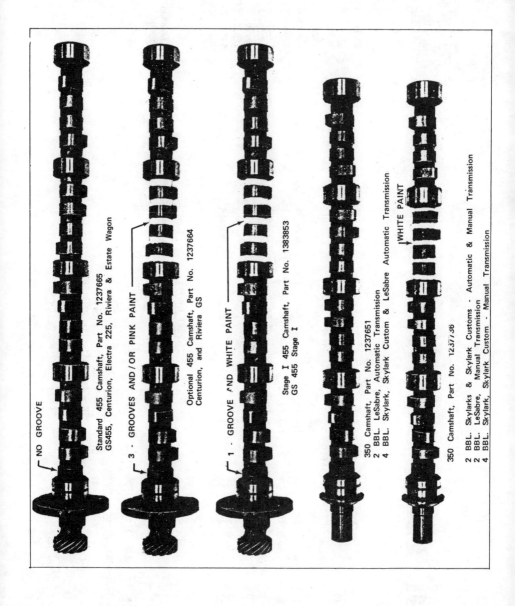

NO GROOVE

Standard 455 Camshaft, Part No. 1237665
GS455, Centurion, Electra 225, Riviera & Estate Wagon

3 - GROOVES AND/OR PINK PAINT

Optional 455 Camshaft, Part No. 1237664
Centurion, and Riviera GS

1 - GROOVE AND WHITE PAINT

Stage I 455 Camshaft, Part No. 1383853
GS 455 Stage I

350 Camshaft, Part No. 1237651
2 BBL. LeSabre, Automatic Transmission
4 BBL. Skylark, Skylark Custom & LeSabre Automatic Transmission

WHITE PAINT

350 Camshaft, Part No. 1237156

2 BBL. Skylarks & Skylark Customs - Automatic & Manual Transmission
2 BBL. LeSabre, Manual Transmission
4 BBL. Skylark, Skylark Custom - Manual Transmission

BUICK MOTOR DIVISION • GENERAL MOTORS CORPORATION • FLINT, MICHIGAN 48550

TO ALL BUICK DEALERS   September 4, 1970

SUBJECT: 1971 Announcement Bulletin

1971 Paint Codes

Color chip sheets for the 1971 Buick paints will again be available from DuPont, Ditzler, and Rinshed-Mason. Each dealer will be sent two copies of each as they are made available to us.

Below is a list of 1971 Buick Exterior Colors.

Paint Code	Sales Code	Color Name	DuPont Stock No.	Ditzler Stock No.	Rinshed-Mason Stock No.
11	C	Artic White	5338L	2058	A-2080
13	P	Platinum Mist	5276L	2327	A-2438
16	L	Tealmist Gray	5324L	2161	A-2472
19	A	Regal Black	99L	9300	A-946
24	D	Cascade Blue	5270L	2328	A-2439
26	B	Stratomist Blue	5327L	2213	A-2262
29	E	Nocturne Blue	5272L	2330	A-2441
39	I	Twilight Turquoise	5277L	2331	A-2442
41	Z	Silver Fern	5282L	2332	A-2443
42	K	Willowmist Green	5274L	2333	A-2444-G
43	H	Lime Mist	5322LH	2334	A-2445-D
49	M	Verdemist Green	5273L	2337	A-2448
50	Y	Bamboo Cream	5342L	2175	A-2270-D
53	Q	Cortez Gold	5280LH	2339	A-2449-F
55	G	Coronet Gold	5326L	2178	A-2479-D
61	W	Sandpiper Beige	5325L	2181	A-2273
62	T	Bittersweet Mist	5281LH	2340	A-2451-G
65	S	Copper Mist	5287L	2343	A-2454-D
67	U	Burnished Cinnamon	5323LH	23215	A-2276-G
68	J	Deep Chestnut	5279L	2344	A-2455
70	F	Pearl Beige	5285L	2346	A-2457
73	V	Sunset Mist	5286L	2347	A-2458
74	X	Vintage Red	5284LM	2348	A-2459-R
75	R	Fire Red	5339LH	2189	A-2278-F
78	N	Rosewood	5275L	2350	A-2461

1971 Month Built Code

The production month built body code appears on the vehicle Protect-O-Plate. The codes for 1971 production are as follows:

January	1	May	5	September	9
February	2	June	6	October	0
March	3	July	7	November	N
April	4	August	8	December	D

Dealer P&A Bulletin

DATE: April 20, 1971

SUBJECT: Octane Adjustment Kits

Unleaded or low-lead gasolines are now being offered to the public by most of the major oil companies.

1970 and prior model Buicks will require modification of the distributor for satisfactory operation on the new fuels. New octane adjustment kits have been developed for this purpose. Each kit will contain distributor springs and/or weights, installation instructions and appropriate label identification to be affixed to the vehicle.

Copies of a manual outlining technical information relative to the modification of engines by the use of these kits are being forwarded to all dealerships by the Buick Service Department under their Bulletin No. 71-I-77 dated April 19, 1971.

General Motors will announce the availability of these kits to all G.M. car owners through a national press release in late April 1971.

The kits will be available through the GMPD Parts Distribution Centers as CX parts and are classified as MF Items. A listing and description of the twelve kits released for modification of Buicks are as follows:

PART NO.	USAGE		SUGGESTED LIST PRICE	GENERAL TRADE	DEALER NET
1951785	1960-63	401 V-8 4-BBL H.C.	$1.90	$1.33	$1.14
1851786	1964-66	401 V-8 4-BBL H.C.	1.90	1.33	1.14
	1964-66	425 V-8 4-BBL H.C.			
1851787	1967-69	430 V-8 4-BBL H.C.	.60	.42	.36
1851788	1970	455 V-8 4-BBL H.C. (First Jobs with Distributor Part No. 1111984)	1.90	1.33	1.14
1851789	1970	455 V-8 4-BBL H.C. (After Jobs with Distributor Part No. 1112027)			

It is suggested that representative stock of these kits be ordered on your next stock order, so that you will be able to provide your customers with this modification.

BUICK DEALER

SERVICE INFORMATION

BULLETIN

Model Year	1971
Bulletin No.	71-I-80
File in Group	00
Number	25
Date	5-14-71

SUBJECT: New Engine Oil Classification System

MODELS AFFECTED:

For the past several years the petroleum industry has been using an API (American Petroleum Institute) service classification system in which letters such as ML, MM, MS designated the service for which engine oils were intended. This API system did not include performance requirements which have become increasingly important for proper engine lubrication and durability.

Oils have been classified and labeled by oil companies for service (such as MS) but the label did not always state whether the oils met car manufacturer's requirements (such as GM 6041-M) as stated in Owner's Manuals. Owners, therefore, could not be sure that they were using engine oil recommended by the vehicle manufacturer.

Both the automobile and petroleum industries recognized these short-comings in the API service classification system, and cooperatively developed a new system which uses a Letter Designation consisting of two letters. The first letter refers to the service for which the oil is intended: "S" indicates passenger car and light truck service; "C" identifies diesel engines and heavy duty gasoline truck service. The second letter identifies the performance level of the oil and its correspondence to performance criteria established by GM and other vehicle manufacturers. Increasing levels of performance are signified by the letters A, B, C, etc.

The Letter Designations for passenger car and light truck service, and their relationship to GM specifications are described in the attached chart. Some oil companies are already marking containers with the new classsification system, while others are converting as existing stocks of containers are depleted.

The Letter Designations do not refer in any way to the viscosity of the oil. As with the previous classification system, a number of single grade and multi-grade oils will be available which meet the performance requirements of each Letter Designation.

GM Owner's Manuals for 1971 passenger cars and light trucks continue to recommend oils meeting the performance requirement of Standard GM 6041-M. This GM specification, however, was updated late in 1970 to require engine oils which better resist thickening during high-speed, high-temperature driving, and are improved in low temperature fluidity.

The Letter Designation "SE" has been established to correspond with the requirements of GM 6041-M as revised, but containers marked "SE" are not expected to appear in any significant quantity until the summer of 1971.

BUICK MOTOR DIVISION   •   SERVICE DEPARTMENT   •   FLINT, MICHIGAN 48550

The "SE" Letter Designation, and not GM 6041-M, will be used in 1972 General Motors Owner's Manuals to recommend engine oil. "SE" engine oils will be better quality and perform better than those identified with "SA" through "SD" designations, and are recommended for all GM passenger cars and light duty gasoline trucks regardless of model year and previous engine oil quality recommendations.

ENGINE OIL PERFORMANCE AND

ENGINE SERVICE CLASSIFICATION SYSTEM

Passenger Cars - Light Trucks

LETTER DESIGNATION	GM SPECIFICATION	APPLICABLE GM MODEL YEAR
SA	None	None
SB	None	None
SC	GM 4745-M	1967 and Prior Years
SD	GM 6041-M (1968 Release)	1970 and Prior Years
SE	GM 6041-M (Revised 1970)	1971 and Prior Years

DATE: April 8, 1971

SUBJECT: Cylinder Heads - 1969-400 & 430 Engines
1970-455 Engines.

Cylinder Head 1231108 is released for 1969 models with 400 and 430 Cu. Inch Engines.

NOTE: The 1969 Engines feed overhead oil through oil galleries in the cylinder block to and through matching feed holes in the cylinder head.

Cylinder Head 1231785 was originally released for 1970 models which feed overhead oil through the push rods. Accordingly, 1970 production engines did not require oil feed holes in the cylinder head.

However, as the only functional difference between the 1969 and 1970 model cylinder heads is the oil feed hole, it was determined all service cylinder heads under part 1231785 would include the oil feed holes, and therefore would service both the 1969 and 1970 models 400, 430 and 455 engines. (Refer to illustration on reverse side.)

The 1969 Cylinder Head 1231108 is now replaced by the 1969-1970 Head 1231785 at most Parts Distribution Centers.

However, we are advised that some 1231785 Heads do not have the holes required for overhead oil feed in the 1969 models.

Please check dealer stocks and receipts of Cylinder Head 1231785 now in transit to you.

1231785 - With oil feed holes - Use 1969-400-430 Engines
and   1970-455 Engines

1231785 - Without oil feed holes - Use 1970-455 Engines only

Tag Dealer Stocks and use accordingly.

NOTE: Use 1969 Head Gaskets as listed for 1969 model engines.
Use 1970 Head Gasket as listed for 1970 model engines.

Parts and Accessories

Specifications and Cataloguing

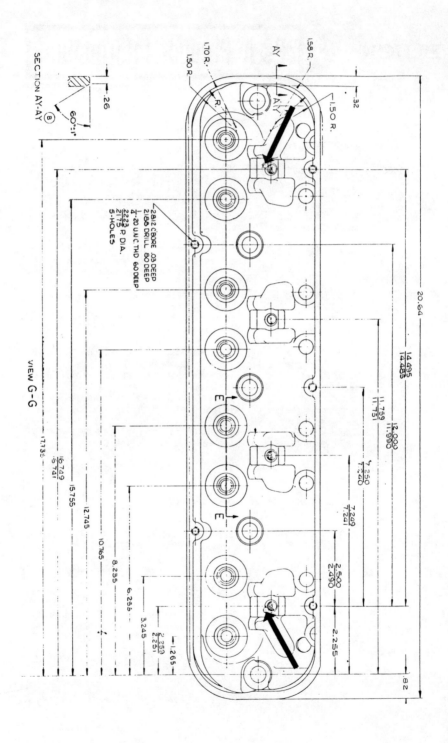

SECTION AY-AY

VIEW G-G

BUICK DEALER

SERVICE INFORMATION

BULLETIN

Model Year	1971
Bulletin No.	71-I-110
File in Group	60
Number	6
Date	8-16-71

SUBJECT: 455 Engine Substitution

MODELS AFFECTED: 1971 Centurions

Approximately 500 Centurions were assembled after July 12, 1971, starting with Vehicle Identification 1X194963 at the Fairfax Assembly Plant with the "TA" coded 455 engine normally used in the performance option (A-9) for this model. The "TA" engine is also used with the Riviera GS option.

This bulletin is being issued to alert dealers to this engine variation so that if a Centurion is brought into a dealership for repairs, correct replacement parts may be ordered by referring to the engine code number.

BUICK MOTOR DIVISION • SERVICE DEPARTMENT • FLINT, MICHIGAN 48550

BUICK DEALER

SERVICE INFORMATION

BULLETIN

Model Year	1971
Bulletin No.	71-I-62
File in Group	60
Number	3
Date	3-5-71

SUBJECT: Engine Oil Pump Pressure Regulator Valve Spring

MODELS AFFECTED: 1971 - 455 Engines

To provide increased oil pressure level for non Stage I
engines, pressure regulator spring (Group 1.609, Part
#1233892) is being installed in the oil pump. This is
the same spring currently being used on Stage I engines.
This spring went into production on all 455 engines on
January 27, 1971, with engine Build code #136.

BUICK DEALER

SERVICE INFORMATION

BULLETIN

Model Year	1971
Bulletin No.	71-I-103
File in Group	60
Number	5
Date	7-5-71

SUBJECT: Removal of Oil Squirt Holes on All Connecting Rods

MODELS AFFECTED: 1971 V-8 Engines

Inquiries have been received concerning the lack of an oil squirt hole on some connecting rods. This oil squirt hole was removed from all connecting rods, both 455 C.I.D. and 350 C.I.D. engines, approximately the first of January, 1971.

Engineering has run many tests and verified that the squirt holes are no longer needed.

NOTE: Bearings or rods with the squirt hole may be used interchangeably for service with the bearings or rods not having the squirt hole.

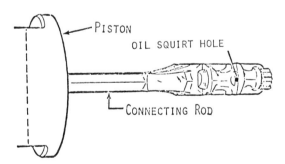

INFORMATION BULLETIN NUMBER
71-I-15

BUICK DEALER
SERVICE INFORMATION
BULLETIN

DEALER FILE	
Model Year	1971
File in Group	130
Number	1

BUICK MOTOR DIVISION • GENERAL MOTORS CORPORATION • FLINT, MICHIGAN 48550

TO ALL BUICK DEALERS

October 9, 1970

SUBJECT: Additional Information on the 1970 and 1971 Buick Engine
Cooling System

The semi-closed engine cooling system was introduced by Buick on its 1970
models and continued on the 1971 models. It has proved very successful,
but may still be misunderstood by a few people.

The system is designed so that the coolant level is easily checked by
merely observing the level in the reservoir container with the coolant
at normal engine operating temperature (hot). Small additions of
coolant (mixture of ethylene glycol and water) are added, when necessary,
to the easily accessible reservoir and not the radiator. See Figure 1.
However, service personnel should be alerted that coolant is not always
added to the reservoir.

When draining and replacing engine coolant every two years, the new
coolant mixture is added directly to the radiator. If a substantial
amount of coolant has been lost or if drained for cooling system repairs,
the coolant mixture is replaced in the radiator. Adding it to the reservoir under these conditions would not place sufficient coolant in the
radiator or engine to sufficiently protect the engine from overheating.

In addition, it is recommended that a coolant sample be taken from the
radiator and not the reservoir when checking coolant for anti-freeze
protection.

Remember, to insure proper sealing of the system, always reinstall the
radiator cap securely and align the stripe on the radiator cap with the
overflow tube. See Figure.

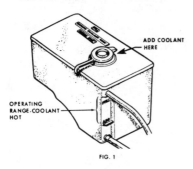

ADD COOLANT
HERE

OPERATING
RANGE-COOLANT
HOT

FIG. 1

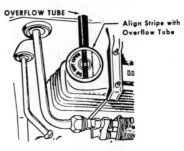

OVERFLOW TUBE

Align Stripe with
Overflow Tube

FIG. 2

BUICK DEALER

SERVICE INFORMATION
BUICK
Authorized
Service

BULLETIN

Model Year	1971
Bulletin No.	71-I-55
File in Group	00
Number	14
Date	2-5-71

SUBJECT: New Heavy-Duty Sealer Now Available - Cooling System
Heavy-Duty Stop Leak, Gr. 8.800, Pt. 1051342

MODELS AFFECTED: All

Now available at GMPD warehouses under Part No. 1051342 is a new
heavy-duty cooling system sealer. This new sealer has been exten-
sively tested and found to be surprisingly effective in sealing
all types of cooling system leaks, including those that cannot be
handled by regular stop-leak products. It is completely compati-
ble with anti-freeze solutions, circulates freely without clogging
or settling, and is designed to be left in the cooling system to
provide residual stop-leak action.

Directions for the proper use of this stop leak are printed on the
label. One 16 oz. can of Part No. 1051342 is sufficient protection
for cooling systems with up to 24 qt. capacity. Buick dealers are
urged to order a supply of this new heavy-duty sealer and to make
it readily available for their service departments.

BUICK MOTOR DIVISION • SERVICE DEPARTMENT • FLINT, MICHIGAN 48550

BUICK DEALER
SERVICE INFORMATION
BULLETIN

BUICK MOTOR DIVISION • GENERAL MOTORS CORPORATION • FLINT, MICHIGAN 48550

November 6, 1970

TO ALL BUICK DEALERS

SUBJECT: Important Characteristics of the 1971 Buick Heaters and Climate Control

MODELS AFFECTED

1971 LeSabres, Estate Wagons, Centurions, Electra 225's and Rivieras

1. Constant Ventilation

   It will be noted that the heater and Climate Control fan switch on the 1971 regular sized Buicks does not have an "OFF" position. This is to insure that the blower fan is constantly providing fresh air ventilation through the passenger compartment. Louvres in the deck lid or Estate Wagon tailgate serve as an air outlet to complete the ventilation cycle.

   To insure passenger comfort in cool weather, the blower fan will not start until engine warm-up with the Selector lever at "OFF" or the Fan switch on "LO". In addition, after engine warm-up with the selector lever in the "OFF" position, the blower is fixed on low speed and the incoming air is discharged under the instrument panel on heater-equipped Buicks and out the heater outlet on air conditioner-equipped Buicks.

2. "DEFOG"

   The operation of the "Defog" and "Deice" positions on the 1971 upper series Climate Control or Automatic Climate Control are new and should be understood by dealer personnel and our customers. Not understanding these new features can result in an erroneous belief that the Climate Control is operating incorrectly.

   Both the 1971 Climate Control and the 1971 Automatic Climate Control units have two settings to remove humidity from the inside of the car windows - "Defog" and "Deice." Their function is as their names imply. The "Deice" operation is basically similar to previous models, except that the air conditioner compressor operates above 35°F. The "Defog" operation is quite different for 1971.

The improved "Defog" operation is as follows:

. Air conditioner compressor is on above 35° F to dry incoming air.

. Incoming dry air is directed through the floor heater outlets, the instrument panel outlets, and a minor portion out the defroster outlets.

. The air out the defroster outlets is delayed from 20 to 60 seconds (early production cars may be longer) so the moist air already in the system can be purged and only dry air is blown onto the windshield.

. Because of the multiple air distribution, side windows as well as the windshield are better defogged.

For severe windshield frosting or icing, set control on "Deice."

Here is a suggestion you might pass on to your customers who purchased 1971 upper series Buicks. The "Defog" position can also serve as an advantageous means of heating or cooling the car's interior. Since, in "Defog", air enters the passenger compartment at three levels simultaneously, floor, instrument panel, and windshield, there is a comfort advantage to be gained by this broader air distribution. The A/C compressor is on above 35° F so the incoming air can be cooled or heat added as desired.

Service Department
BUICK MOTOR DIVISION
Flint, Michigan 48550

187

BUICK DEALER

SERVICE INFORMATION

BULLETIN

Model Year	1971
Bulletin No.	71-I-82
File in Group	00
Number	27
Date	5-14-71

SUBJECT: Electronic Communication Equipment Used on Vehicles with Max Trac

MODELS AFFECTED: 1971 45, 46, 48 and 49000 Series with Max Trac

In 1971 Buick has offered an option called Max Trac. This system electronically compares front and rear wheel speed signals and limits engine power to avoid excessive rear wheel "spin." There has been considerable feed back from the owners questioning the effect of other electronic communications equipment, such as mobile phones and two-way radios, on the operation of Max Trac.

Testing indicates that if the antenna and lead in for other electronic equipment is at least 3 feet from the Max Trac controller (right end of instrument panel), no problem will be encountered with the Max Trac System. Testing also indicates that the three foot distance is conservative. The 1971 LeSabre, Centurion, Electra and Riviera Car Owner's Manuals have a note in the Max Trac section spelling out the 3 foot requirement.

If there is any question as to the affect of auxiliary electronic communications equipment on Max Trac, this can be easily checked. Turn Max Trac system "on." While accelerating normally, (do not spin rear wheels) make a radio transmission. If there is no noticeable reduction in engine output during the transmission, one can assume that the auxiliary electronic equipment has no affect on the operation of Max Trac.

VEHICLE INFORMATIVE & CAUTIONARY LABELS

LABEL	LOCATION	SKYLARK	LeSABRE & CENTURION	ELECTRA	RIVIERA
RECOMMENDED OIL CHANGE	Left Front Fender Skirt	734791	734791	734791	734791
ENGINE ADJUSTMENTS	Radiator Tie Panel				
250 C.T.		3994010			
250 A.T.		3994010			
350 2 bbl. C.T.		1237190	1237190		
350 2 bbl. A.T.		1237191	1237191		
350 2 bbl. W/H.D. Cooling		1237192	1237192		
350 2 bbl. W/A.C.		1237193	1237193		
350 4 bbl. W/A.C.		1237194	1237194		
350 4 bbl. Less A.C.		1237195	1237195		
455 All Except Stage 1		1237199	1237199	1237199	1237199
455 Stage 1		1237198			
CARBURETOR ADJUSTMENT	Radiator Tie Panel	1238411	1238411	1238411	1238411
ENGINE IDENTIFICATION	Air Cleaner				
350-2		1231284	1231284		
350-4 Std. Comp.		1231285	1231285		
350-4 High Comp.		1234413	1234413		
GS 350		1234653			
455-4		1232909	1232909	1232909	1232909
Stage 1		1234370			
GS 455		1234652			
TIRE PRESSURE	Glove Box Door				
Except Wagons & GS		1238959	1238962	1238962	1238962
Wagons		1238961	1238963		
GS		1238960			1238962
JACK INSTRUCTIONS					
Except Wagons	Trunk Lid	1237711	1237108	1237108	1237878
Wagons	Rear Compartment	1237912	1237109		
Convertibles	Trunk Lid		1237797		
SPARE TIRE & JACK STOWAGE	Trunk Lid	1234906	1237108	1237108	1237878

ORDER BY PART NUMBER FROM --

BUICK MOTOR DIVISION
P & A MERCHANDISING DEPT.
FLINT, MICHIGAN 48550

DO NOT ORDER THROUGH GMPD.

BUICK DEALER
SERVICE INFORMATION
BULLETIN

BUICK MOTOR DIVISION • **GENERAL MOTORS CORPORATION** • **FLINT, MICHIGAN 48550**

TO ALL BUICK DEALERS   October 9, 1970

SUBJECT: Combination Valve - All Models With Disc Brakes

All 1971 model Buicks, except drum brake Skylarks, will be equipped with a newly-developed "Combination Valve" in the hydraulic brake apply system. See Figure 1. As the name implies, this device combines several functions which, on previous disc brake cars, were accomplished by separate units located throughout the hydraulic system. These functions are:

1. Metering Valve - used to achieve a uniform starting pressure for front and rear brakes.

2. Brake Warning Switch - replacing the previous switch and junction block assembly--with added automatic reset features.

   NOTE: The 1971 Brake Warning Switch has an automatic reset feature that is different from 1970. When a brake failure occurs on a 1971 model, the warning light will come on and stay on until the system is repaired. After the system is repaired, stepping on the brake will shut the light off.

3. Proportioning Valve - used to achieve optimum balance between front and rear brakes for various levels of braking.

4. Proportioner Bypass - a new function which reduces pedal effort in the event of a front brake system hydraulic leak.

To achieve the desired functional characteristics of the proportioning valve, (item 3 above) it is necessary to expose one side of a piston to atmospheric pressure. Thus, a small chamber within the valve body is vented to atmosphere. Since all moving seals pass traces of the fluid they seal, in due time this fluid may appear at the atmospheric vent.

In the case of Bendix and Delco Moraine units, the vent is through the threads of the large plug in the rear of the valve body. In the Kelsey-Hayes unit, the vent is in the large plug on the bottom boss of the valve body. See Figure 2.

Traces of dampness at these vent locations may be safely ignored. However, if a drop of fluid is noted, or there is appreciable wetness in the area, check the level of fluid in the rear master cylinder reservoir. If fluid level is more than 1/2 inch below the top of the reservoir and no other fluid leaks are noted in the hydraulic system, the combination valve assembly should be replaced. No attempt should be made to disassemble or repair the combination valve. If the valve fails, the complete assembly should be replaced.

Service Department
BUICK MOTOR DIVISION
Flint, Michigan 48550

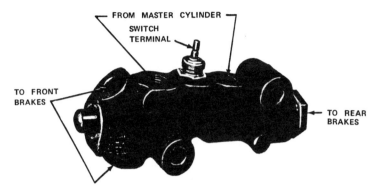

FROM MASTER CYLINDER

SWITCH
TERMINAL

TO FRONT
BRAKES

TO REAR
BRAKES

DISC BRAKES COMBINATION VALVE
DELCO MORAINE SHOWN

FIGURE 1

ATMOSPHERIC VENT IS THROUGH THREADS OF THE
LARGE PLUG IN THE REAR OF THE VALVE BODY

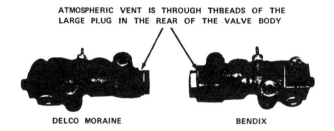

DELCO MORAINE   BENDIX

KELSEY-HAYES

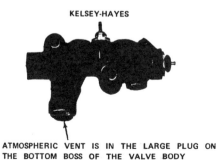

ATMOSPHERIC VENT IS IN THE LARGE PLUG ON
THE BOTTOM BOSS OF THE VALVE BODY

FIGURE 2

BUICK DEALER
SERVICE INFORMATION
BULLETIN

BUICK MOTOR DIVISION • GENERAL MOTORS CORPORATION • FLINT, MICHIGAN 48550

TO ALL BUICK DEALERS
October 9, 1970

SUBJECT: 1971 Wiring Harness Repair - 45-46-48-49000 Series

To improve body wiring installations and reduce the most common electrical failures such as pinches, screws driven into the wiring and disconnected connectors, a new type of wiring harness construction is being introduced for 1971. This new construction has a solid copper core wire rather than stranded wire. A thinner, harder and tougher insulation, it is further protected with a jacketed conduit and has a self-rejecting connector at the rear.

The entire harness results in a smaller, tougher and more reliable wiring system which fits more easily into the confined space available in a car.

The maintenance and repair of this harness requires the same good common sense practices as used in the past to repair electrical wiring plus a few special techniques required to ensure a permanent and reliable electrical system.

Some precautions that are necessary when repairing solid core wiring harnesses are:

1. Extra care must be exercised in stripping so that the core of the wire is neither cut or nicked. (Nicked or cut solid core wire will break easily.)

2. All joints to the copper core _must_ be soldered.

3. Apply at least two layers of electrical tape over the splice.

4. A splice should be located in straight sections of the wiring and not in areas of bends or pinches.

Service Department
BUICK MOTOR DIVISION
Flint, Michigan 48550

BUICK DEALER
SERVICE INFORMATION
BULLETIN

BUICK MOTOR DIVISION • GENERAL MOTORS CORPORATION • FLINT, MICHIGAN 48550

October 30, 1970

TO ALL BUICK DEALERS

SUBJECT: New Rear Accumulator Piston Containing a Teflon Oil Seal Ring

MODELS AFFECTED: All 1971 Models Equipped with the Turbo Hydra-matic "400" Transmission

The 1971 THM-400 Transmission is now being built with a new (2nd type) rear accumulator piston containing a teflon oil seal ring in the large diameter ring groove. See illustration. The piston can be identified by the number 8627200 cast in the piston. The 2nd type piston large diameter ring groove is machined shallower than the 1st type piston, which used an aluminum ring. Therefore, the teflon ring is not interchangeable with the aluminum ring. The small diameter ring groove and oil seal ring have not been changed.

The beginning transmission serial numbers and build date codes of transmissions containing the new 2nd type piston and teflon oil seal ring are as follows:

Transmission Serial Numbers	Build Date Codes
71-BA-1536	224
71-BB-1001	Start of Production
71-BC-19421	245
71-BT-2250	245

SERVICE INFORMATION

As an assembly, with the correct rings installed, the 1st and 2nd type rear accumulator pistons are interchangeable.

The following parts are serviced:

Part Name		Group No.	Part No.
Rear Accumulator Piston	(1st Type)	4.241	8623669
Aluminum Oil Seal Ring	(Large Dia.)	4.242	8623672
Aluminum Oil Seal Ring	(Small Dia.)	4.242	8623671
Teflon Oil Seal Ring	(Large Dia.)	4.242	8627153

Service Department
BUICK MOTOR DIVISION
Flint, Michigan 48550

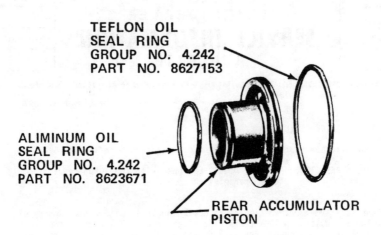

TEFLON OIL
SEAL RING
GROUP NO. 4.242
PART NO. 8627153

ALIMINUM OIL
SEAL RING
GROUP NO. 4.242
PART NO. 8623671

REAR ACCUMULATOR
PISTON

1971 THM-400 2ND TYPE
REAR ACCUMULATOR PISTON

BUICK DEALER

SERVICE INFORMATION

BULLETIN

Model Year	1972
Bulletin No.	72-I-2
File in Group	00
Number	2
Date	8-27-71

SUBJECT: 1972 Announcement Bulletin

MODELS AFFECTED: All 1972 Buicks

Paint Code	Sales Code	Color Name	Du Pont Stock No.	Ditzler Stock No.	Rinshed-Mason Stock No.
11	C	Artic White	5338L	2058	A-2080
14	V	Silver Mist	5426L	2429	A-2541
18	W	Charcoal Mist	5427L	2430	A-2542
19	A	Regal Black	99L	9300	A-946
21	D	Chrystal Blue	5440L	2431	A-2543
24	T	Cascade Blue	5464L	2328	A-2576
26	B	Stratomist Blue	5327L	2213	A-2482
28	E	Royal Blue	5124L	2166	A-2264
36	H	Heritage Green	5436L	2433	A-2546D
43	F	Seamist Green	5428L	2435	A-2548
45	G	Emerald Mist	5463L	2172	A-2577
48	I	Hunter Green	5429L	2439	A-2552
50	J	Sandalwood	5431L	2441	A-2554
53	Q	Cortez Gold	5469L	2339	A-2578F
54	S	Champagne Gold	5432L	2442	A-2556D
56	Y	Sunburst Yellow	5443L	2444	A-2558G
57	U	Antique Gold	5439L	2445	A-2559
62	L	Sierra Tan	5437L	2447	A-2561
63	M	Burnished Copper	5434L	2448	A-2562D
65	Z	Flame Orange	5435L	2450	A-2564D
67	K	Deep Chestnut	5279L	2344	A-2455
69	N	Nutmeg	5438L	2452	A-2566
73	X	Vintage Red	5284L	2348	A-2459R
75	R	Fire Red	5339L	2189	A-2278F
77	P	Burnished Bronze	5425L	2454	A-2568F

	BUICK DEALER	Model Year	1972
	SERVICE INFORMATION	Bulletin No.	72-I-69
Authorized Service		File in Group	00
	BULLETIN	Number	10
		Date	4-25-72

SUBJECT: Revisions to 1972 Buick Chassis Service Manual

MODELS	ENGINE	TRANSMISSION	STANDARD			ECONOMY			PERFORMANCE		
			RATIO	REGULAR CODE	LIMITED SLIP CODE	RATIO	(G95) REGULAR CODE	(G96) LIMITED SLIP CODE	RATIO	(G92) REGULAR CODE	(G91) LIMITED SLIP CODE
CENTURION	455	THM 400	2.93	QW	QY						
RIVIERA GS	455	THM 400	3.42		QA						
LE SABRE OR CENTURION	455	THM-400	2.93	QT	QJ						
RIVIERA	455	THM-400	2.73	QP	QS				2.93	QI	QJ
ELECTRA	455	THM-400	2.73	QP	QS				2.93	QI	QJ
CENTURION	455	THM-400	2.93	QI	QJ				3.42	QT	QA
ESTATE WAGON	455	THM-400	2.93	QE	QL				3.42	QH	QM
LE SABRE	455	THM-400	2.93	QI	QJ				3.42	QT	QA
LE SABRE	350	THM-350 [1]	3.08	NAC / NAB	NP	2.73	NK		3.42	NHB	NSB

*Police Car Option

FIGURE 40-144 (REVISED)

40-251A

197

BUICK DEALER

SERVICE INFORMATION

BULLETIN

Model Year	1972
Bulletin No.	72-I-92
File in Group	BODY
Number	24
Date	7-5-72

SUBJECT: 3-Point Lap/Shoulder Belt Restraint System

MODELS AFFECTED: Late Production 1972's

This bulletin is presented to discuss the function and background of the new restraint system described in Information Bulletin 72-I-36, Body #5, dated January 18, 1972.

The new belt system was introduced to meet the requirements of the Federal Motor Vehicle Safety Standards. Effective January 1, 1972, the National Highway Traffic Safety Administration (NHTSA) amended Standard 208 for the purpose of increasing the use of both the lap and shoulder belt. The intention of the standard was first, to make the lap/shoulder belt easier to use by having both attached to a single buckle, and second, to encourage their use by means of a light and buzzer reminder.

To reduce the possibility of injury in a collision from the belt itself, the standard also specifies that the attachment point of the shoulder belt to the lap belt be located at least six inches off of the center of an average-size occupant. The reason for this is that in frontal type accidents there may be a tendency for the shoulder belt to pull the lap belt up over the strong pelvic structure (hip bones) of the human body into the relatively weak abdominal area (the stomach). To reduce this possibility, the attachment of the shoulder belt to the lap belt must be located to one side.

It is this requirement that is making the buckling operation more inconvenient for some Buick owners. In our former system where the lap and shoulder belts were not attached to each other, the lap belt buckle could be centrally located.

We should add that some of our owners who were at first troubled by the new system now report that they have become use to it and are using the lap/shoulder system for the first time. The reason most often given is that the retractor pulls both belts out of the way at the same time when they are connected. These same people find they have no stowage problem and always know exactly where to find the belts when they re-enter the car. By turning slightly toward the buckle they find it easier to fasten. When they move back to the straight-ahead position, the self-locking retractor adjusts the lap belt automatically.

Please review this information with your Sales and Service personnel so that they are prepared to discuss this subject with Buick owners when inquiries are received.

BUICK MOTOR DIVISION   •   SERVICE DEPARTMENT   •   FLINT, MICHIGAN 48550

BUICK
Authorized
Service

BUICK DEALER

SERVICE INFORMATION

BULLETIN

Model Year	1972
Bulletin No.	72-I-72
File in Group	68
Number	9
Date	5-9-72

SUBJECT: Distributor Point and Condenser Change

MODELS AFFECTED: 1972 Late Production Models

Some distributors used in 1972 production Buick engines will
utilize a new combination point-condenser unit. This unit
provides improved interference suppression and eliminates
the need for the shield surrounding the points. New point
condenser assembly units will fit 1972 and earlier distributors. However, when replacing the points and condenser
on earlier models with this new type assembly, the suppression
shield (used on 1970 and 1971 models) can be eliminated.

Note: Early type points and condensers will not fit the
late model 1972 distributors.

IMPORTANT

All point condenser units, Part #1975000, that have been
replaced in warranty, as defective parts, should be returned
to Buick's Clear Signal Area per instructions shown in
Buick Service Information Bulletin 72-I-12B, File Group 00,
No. 7B.

The illustration below shows the new combination point
condenser unit as compared to the two pieces used previously.

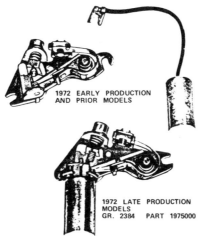

1972 EARLY PRODUCTION
AND PRIOR MODELS

1972 LATE PRODUCTION
MODELS
GR. 2384   PART 1975000

BUICK MOTOR DIVISION • **SERVICE DEPARTMENT** • **FLINT, MICHIGAN 48550**

BUICK DEALER

SERVICE INFORMATION

BULLETIN

Model Year	1972
Bulletin No.	72-I-60
File in Group	64
Number	2
Date	3-28-72

SUBJECT: Fuel Recommendations

MODELS AFFECTED: All 1971 and 1972 Buicks

Beginning with the 1971 model, all Buicks have been designed to operate on unleaded or low-lead gasolines.

The use of unleaded or low-lead fuels of at least 91 Research Octane Number should be encouraged for the following reasons:

. reduces hydrocarbon emissions,
. increases spark plug and exhaust system life,
. reduces contamination of lubricating oil,
. reduces valve deposits and prolongs valve life.

Lead in fuel can cause deposits to form on the valve face which, if excessive, may prevent the valve from seating and could result in burned valves. 1971-72 engines have exhaust valves which are nickel plated to minimize wear when operated on unleaded or low-lead fuels.

Premium fuels contain about 2.5 grams of lead per gallon and regular, fuels contain about 2.0 grams of lead per gallon. Low-lead fuels contain about 0.5 gram of lead per gallon while unleaded fuels do not have any lead added during the manufacturing process.

Therefore, unleaded or low-lead fuels are recommended for use in all 1971 and 1972 Buick passenger cars. If unleaded or low-lead gasolines are not available, regular fuels may be used.

All 1971-72 Buick owners should be made aware of the unleaded and low-lead fuel recommendations at the time of new vehicle delivery, or whenever a vehicle is brought in for service.

PLEASE ASK YOUR SALES AND SERVICE MANAGEMENT TO COVER THE ABOVE INFORMATION WITH ALL DEALERSHIP SALES AND SERVICE PERSONNEL.

BUICK

Authorized Service

BUICK DEALER

SERVICE INFORMATION

BULLETIN

Model Year	1972
Bulletin No.	72-I-42
File in Group	120
Number	7
Date	2-1-72

SUBJECT: Maintenance Free Battery

MODELS AFFECTED: 1972 Riviera - Option

This optional Energizer is sealed so that the electrolite level need not be checked nor added during the normal life of the energizer.

Since the specific gravity of the electrolite cannot be checked with a hydrometer, if this energizer is discharged or suspected of having a low charge, follow the new charging and inspection procedure below.

Charging Instructions:

1. Charge at maximum setting of charger for the length of time shown below:

Initial Charge Rate*	Time to Charge
75 amps.	40 min.
50 amps.	1 hour
25 amps.	2 hours
10 amps.	5 hours

* Initial charge rate is the current that the Energizer will accept at the start of charging. As the Energizer is charged, this rate will decrease.

When a charger does not have an ammeter, place a test ammeter in series with the charger to determine the initial charge rate.

If Energizer temperature is 32° F or less, Energizer should be charged for 1/2 hour at charger's highest setting before the charge rate is determined.

2. Do not exceed the calculated hours of charge, as overheating and spewing of acid might result. In case of spewing, shut off the charger and proceed with testing.

Testing Procedures

The following warranty check procedure has been established for the Maintenance-Free Energizer. The load test in this procedure has been designed in order to determine the difference between an Energizer that has failed and one that is discharged.

1. Visual Inspection

Check for obvious damage, such as a cracked or broken case, that could permit loss of electrolyte. If obvious physical damage is noted, replace Energizer.

BUICK MOTOR DIVISION • SERVICE DEPARTMENT • FLINT, MICHIGAN 48550

2. Preparation

   (a) If no physical damage is noted, charge Energizer per the
        Maintenance-Free Energizer Charging instructions.

   (b) After charging, connect a 300 ampere load across terminals
        for 15 seconds to remove surface charge from Energizer.

3. Load Test

   (a) Connect voltmeter and 230 ampere load across terminals.

   (b) Read voltage after 15 seconds with load connected, then
        disconnect load.

   (c) If voltage is at or below the minimum in the chart below,
        replace the Energizer.

	70° F and Above	60°F	50°F	40°F	30°F	20°F	10°F	0°F
Minimum Voltage	9.6	9.5	9.4	9.3	9.1	8.9	8.7	8.5

Model Year	1972
Bulletin No.	72-I-101
File in Group	90
Number	4
Date	7-25-72

SUBJECT: Power Steering Fluid Usage

MODELS AFFECTED: All

Reports from dealers indicate there is some confusion concerning the use of power steering fluid Group 8.800, Part No. 1050017 and Dexron automatic transmission fluid in power steering pumps.

Small additions of Dexron fluid to maintain the proper pump level do not adversely affect the overall performance of the steering system, but complete replacement with Dexron should be avoided.

Buicks recommendations are as follows:

1. Use power steering fluid in all cases, if possible.

2. If power steering fluid is not availible, Dexron may be used to maintain the proper pump fluid level.

3. In cases where most of the oil must be replaced (flushing the system, major overhauls, etc.), only power steering fluid should be used.

BUICK DEALER

SERVICE TECHNICAL

BULLETIN

Model Year	1972
Bulletin No.	72-T-39
File in Group	64
Number	4
Date	10-24-72

SUBJECT: Fuel Vapor Lock During Heavy Duty Operation

MODELS AFFECTED: 1971 and 1972 45, 46, 48 and 49000 Series

CONDITION:

Engine stalls, runs rough and surges during heavy duty operation in hot weather

The above symptoms may be encountered on a vehicle pulling a trailer at high altitudes during hot weather. This condition may be due to fuel vapor lock aggravated by engine heat being trasferred into the fuel system.

CORRECTION:

I. 350 LeSabre
    1. Remove clip and cut metal fuel line(s) 1 1/4" outboard of left side clip on rear side of front crossmember as shown in Figure 1. Discard front pipe section(s) and hose(s) to fuel pump inlet. Deburr new pipe ends.

CAUTION:

Inspect brake pipe after fuel line has been cut to be sure no damage resulted from this operation.

    2. Install 17" long 3/8" I.D. rubber fuel hose and 17" long 1/4" I.D. rubber fuel return hose (when equipped with fuel return) using clamps, Group 1.166, Part #2492772, at shortened pipe end(s).

    3. Route rubber hose(s) through opening in left side engine mounting bracket as shown. Use new hose clamp(s) (Group 1.166, Part #2494772) at pump inlet.

II 455 Upper Series
    1. Remove and replace production fuel pump with "deep cover" fuel pump, Group 3.900, Part #6470098, presently used on GS 455 engines.

    2. Cut the metal fuel line from the fuel pump to carburetor at the location shown in Figure 2. Install a piece of 4" rubber fuel line, Group 8.962, Part 9432963 and secure with two (2) screw type clamps, Group 8.948, Part 2494772 (1/4" to 5/8" size.)

    3. Cup approximately 1 1/2" off of the rubber fuel feed and fuel return lines and reconnect to fuel pump.

WARRANTY DOCUMENT INFORMATION:

When submitting a warranty document for the work performed in this bulletin, use claim code 92. The labor operations and flat rate times are as follows:

LeSabre - 350 Engine	J093900	.4 hr.
45, 46, 48 and 49000 Series 455 Engines	J093800	.6 hr.

BUICK MOTOR DIVISION • **SERVICE DEPARTMENT** • **FLINT, MICHIGAN 48550**

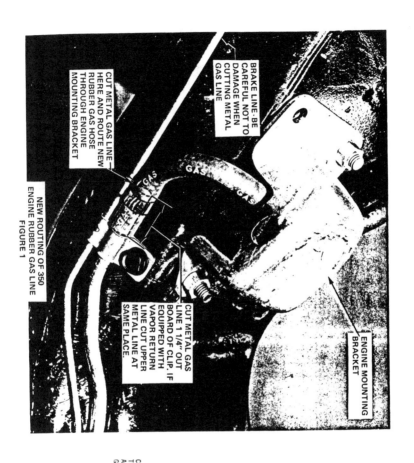

BRAKE LINE: BE
CAREFUL NOT TO
DAMAGE WHEN
CUTTING METAL
GAS LINE

CUT METAL GAS LINE
HERE AND ROUTE NEW
RUBBER GAS HOSE
THROUGH ENGINE
MOUNTING BRACKET

CUT METAL GAS
LINE 1 1/4" OUT
BOARD OF CLIP, IF
EQUIPPED WITH
VAPOR RETURN
LINE CUT UPPER
METAL LINE AT
SAME PLACE.

ENGINE MOUNTING
BRACKET

NEW ROUTING OF 350
ENGINE RUBBER GAS LINE
FIGURE 1

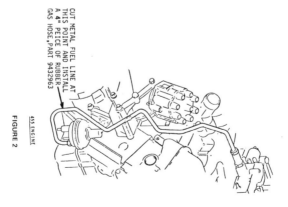

CUT METAL FUEL LINE AT
THIS POINT AND INSTALL
A 4" PEICE OF RUBBER
GAS HOSE, PART 9432963

455 ENGINE

FIGURE 2

205

BUICK DEALER

SERVICE INFORMATION

BULLETIN

Model Year	1972
Bulletin No.	72-I-55
File in Group	40
Number	6
Date	3-6-72

SUBJECT: Proper Rear Axle Lubricant Level

MODELS AFFECTED: All 1972 Models

This bulletin is being issued to help clarify the correct axle lube level of 1972 Buicks.

All models, except Estate Wagons, should be filled flush to 3/8" below the filler plug. Estate Wagons should be flush to 3/4" below filler hole.

BUICK MOTOR DIVISION   •   SERVICE DEPARTMENT   •   FLINT, MICHIGAN 48550

BUICK DEALER

SERVICE INFORMATION

BULLETIN

Model Year	1972
Bulletin No.	72-I-66
File in Group	30
Number	2
Date	4-5-72

SUBJECT: Front Wheel Hub Inner Bearing Seal Installation

MODELS AFFECTED: 1971 and 1972 - 45, 46, 48 and 49000 Series

Improper installation of the front wheel hub inner bearing seal can cause a grease leak, if the seal is driven too deep into the hub. The correct installation of the seal is flush to .010" below the hub surface. The following illustration shows the proper position of the seal in the hub.

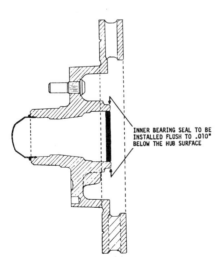

INNER BEARING SEAL TO BE INSTALLED FLUSH TO .010" BELOW THE HUB SURFACE

FRONT WHEEL HUB WITH BEARING INSTALLED

BUICK MOTOR DIVISION • SERVICE DEPARTMENT • FLINT, MICHIGAN 48550

BUICK DEALER

SERVICE TECHNICAL

BULLETIN

Model Year	1972
Bulletin No.	72-T-19
File in Group	120
Number	11
Date	3-28-72

SUBJECT: Voltage Regulator Noise in Radios

MODELS AFFECTED: 1972 Rivieras

CONDITION:

Voltage regulator noise being transmitted through radio on some 1972 Rivieras. Noise is identifiable as a "whine" on AM band (weak station) and disappears when headlights are turned on.

CORRECTION:

Install a 0.5 MFD capacitor, Group 2.480, Part No. 8904366. The capacitor plugs into the fuse block "ACC" terminal. It is attached to the brake pedal bracket by a #8 - 18 x 3/8" (bright metal) washer-head screw for ground purposes.

NOTE: Vehicles with serial numbers greater than 2H917000 already have the capacitor installed in production.

PARTS INFORMATION:

Group No.	Part No.	Dealer Price		25% of Dealer Price		Total
2.480	8904366	$2.32	+	$.57	=	$2.89

WARRANTY DOCUMENT INFORMATION:

When submitting a warranty document for the operation above, use Claim Code 092, Labor Operation J093500 and suggested flat rate time of .2 hr.

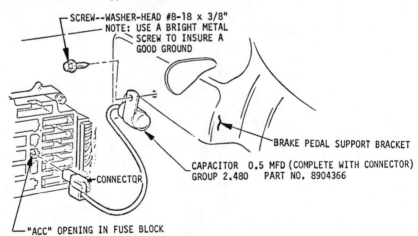

SCREW--WASHER-HEAD #8-18 x 3/8"
NOTE: USE A BRIGHT METAL SCREW TO INSURE A GOOD GROUND

BRAKE PEDAL SUPPORT BRACKET

CAPACITOR 0.5 MFD (COMPLETE WITH CONNECTOR)
GROUP 2.480   PART NO. 8904366

CONNECTOR

"ACC" OPENING IN FUSE BLOCK

BUICK MOTOR DIVISION   •   SERVICE DEPARTMENT   •   FLINT, MICHIGAN 48550

BUICK DEALER

SERVICE INFORMATION

BULLETIN

Model Year	1972
Bulletin No.	72-I-12
File in Group	68
Number	1
Date	10-18-71

SUBJECT: Replacing Rectifier Bridge on Delcotron[R] Generator

MODELS AFFECTED: 1972 Rivieras

The 1972 Buick Riviera Delcotrons have been built with two (2) types of rectifier bridges. The basic difference between the two rectifiers is the type of insulators used.

The first type rectifier uses two separate round insulator washers, whereas the second type has a built in insulator as part of the rectifier. Refer to Figures 1 and 2.

The second type rectifier, Group 2.319, Part #1852209, is the only one available for Service replacement. When replacing a first type rectifier with the second type, the round insulator washers must be removed and discarded prior to assembly of the rectifier.

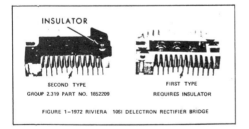

INSULATOR

SECOND TYPE
GROUP 2.319 PART NO. 1852209

FIRST TYPE
REQUIRES INSULATOR

FIGURE 1—1972 RIVIERA 10SI DELECTRON RECTIFIER BRIDGE

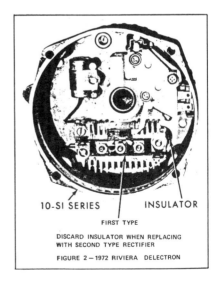

10-SI SERIES   INSULATOR

FIRST TYPE

DISCARD INSULATOR WHEN REPLACING
WITH SECOND TYPE RECTIFIER

FIGURE 2 — 1972 RIVIERA DELECTRON

BUICK MOTOR DIVISION • SERVICE DEPARTMENT • FLINT, MICHIGAN 48550

BUICK DEALER

SERVICE INFORMATION

BULLETIN

Model Year	1972
Bulletin No.	72-I-27
File in Group	64
Number	1
Date	12-10-71

SUBJECT: 1972 Emission Controls

MODELS AFFECTED: All 1972's

All 1972 Buick engines are built in the Engine Plant at Flint and shipped to an Assembly Plant for installation in the automobile.

Rochester Division calibrates the carburetors on an intricate flow bench to a pre-scribed air fuel ratio that will meet all emission requirements at the specified rpm.

Carburetors are audited daily by Rochester Division which assures us of having properly adjusted and calibrated carburetors to install on all engines produced.

Engine timing is adjusted at a specified engine rpm to the Specifications which are listed in the Emission Test Procedure and which comply with the Federal Regulations. Monitoring of this system shows that the timing is set to these specifications at nearly a 100% rate. <u>No further adjustments to carburetors or timing are made in production.</u>

On a brand new automobile, as delivered to the dealer, the engine rpm may be below the service specification; but after a few hundred miles break-in, the engine rpm increases to the service specification. Also some engine roughness at idle may be noticed. This improves with break-in mileage.

It should be emphasized that the technician make no changes on these production settings while performing the new vehicle inspection. The only exception to this would be when the performance of the vehicle is completely unacceptable as deter-mined by a road test or when a correction to a specific condition is issued in a Dealer Service Bulletin.

It is important that you solicit equipment suppliers to periodically check your equipment for correct calibration. This is especially true of a tachometer and timing light which are very important in controlling emissions. Spot checks of tachometer and timing lights show a high percentage reading incorrectly.

Emphasizing and reviewing these steps with your technicians will help in making sure that your dealership will continue to lead in the control of emissions.

BUICK MOTOR DIVISION • **SERVICE DEPARTMENT** • **FLINT, MICHIGAN 48550**

BUICK DEALER

SERVICE INFORMATION

BULLETIN

Model Year	1972
Bulletin No.	72-I-98
File in Group	BODY
Number	27
Date	7-18-72

SUBJECT: Electrodeposited Prime Paint on Service Sheet Metal

MODELS AFFECTED:

Service sheet metal is prime painted at the Parts Warehouse by an electrodeposited prime paint process. The electrodeposited prime paint offers advantages in a more uniform prime coating thickness, no sags, no fatty edges or washed out areas. The primer is readily recognized by its black uniform glossy appearance.

To assure good color finish quality of parts that have electrodeposited prime paint, it is important that the following be performed:

1. The electrodeposited prime coat MUST BE LIGHTLY and CAREFULLY scuff sanded and solvent wiped prior to any subsequent paint application. Sanding through the primer into bare metal will impair the ultimate quality of the finish and should be avoided.

2. An application of sealer or primer surfacer is required prior to acrylic top coat.

BUICK DEALER

SERVICE INFORMATION

BULLETIN

Model Year	1972
Bulletin No.	72-I-50
File in Group	40
Number	4
Date	2-22-72

SUBJECT: Noise Incorrectly Diagnosed As Rear Axle Whine

MODELS AFFECTED: 1972 Buick LeSabres, Centurions, Electras and Rivieras

1972 Buick LeSabres, Centurions, Electras and Rivieras may be encountered with a "high pitched whine" type of noise.

The noise is sensitive to car speed but not engine load or throttle opening, however, it can easily be mis-diagnosed as rear axle gear or bearing noise.

Before attempting any axle corrective work for noise complaints, it is advisable to spin each front wheel with a wheel balancer motor to make sure the noise is not coming from the front wheel.

BUICK DEALER

SERVICE TECHNICAL

BULLETIN

Model Year	1972
Bulletin No.	72-T-32
File in Group	75
Number	11
Date	7-5-72

SUBJECT: Improper 3-2 Downshifts

MODELS AFFECTED: 1971 and 1972 THM 400 Automatic Transmissions

Owner complaints of early or no 3-2 downshifts on a THM 400 transmission may be due to an incorrect adjustment of the detent switch or the switch being positioned out of its adjustment range.

When investigating for the cause of this condition, first adjust the detent switch by pushing switch slide all the way up toward engine compartment bulkhead, then depress accelerator lever all the way down to the floor pan, this automatically sets switch. See Figure 1.

NOTE: Detent switch must be adjusted with accessory floor mat in place.

If the accelerator lever causes the switch slide to bottom out and puts a strain on the bracket at full throttle, the transmission detent solenoid may be energized too soon causing an early downshift. To correct this problem carefully bend the switch bracket <u>down</u> as required, see Figure 2, and re-adjust the switch.

If the switch slide has too little travel at full throttle position, no 3-2 shift can occur. To correct this condition carefully bend the switch bracket <u>up</u> as required, see Figure 3, and re-adjust the switch.

WARRANTY DOCUMENT INFORMATION

When submitting a warranty document for the work performed in this bulletin, use Claim Code 92, Labor Operation K091700 and Flat Rate time of .2 hr.

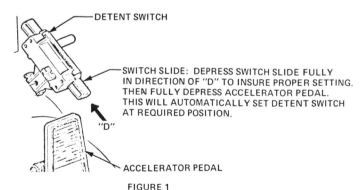

FIGURE 1

ADJUSTING DETENT SWITCH

BUICK MOTOR DIVISION • SERVICE DEPARTMENT • FLINT, MICHIGAN 48550

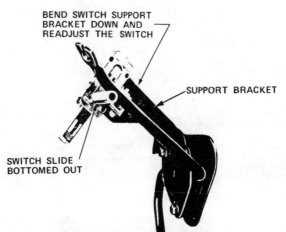

BEND SWITCH SUPPORT
BRACKET DOWN AND
READJUST THE SWITCH

SUPPORT BRACKET

SWITCH SLIDE
BOTTOMED OUT

DETENT SWITCH BOTTOMS OUT AT FULL
THROTTLE AND ENGAGES TOO EARLY
FIGURE 2

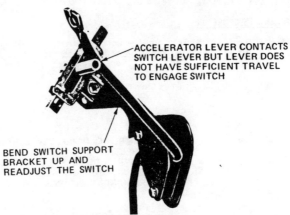

ACCELERATOR LEVER CONTACTS
SWITCH LEVER BUT LEVER DOES
NOT HAVE SUFFICIENT TRAVEL
TO ENGAGE SWITCH

BEND SWITCH SUPPORT
BRACKET UP AND
READJUST THE SWITCH

TOO LITTLE TRAVEL
AT SWITCH AT FULL THROTTLE
FIGURE 3

BUICK
Authorized
Service

BUICK DEALER

SERVICE TECHNICAL
BULLETIN

Model Year	1972
Bulletin No.	72-T-31A
File in Group	75
Number	8A
Date	12-5-72

SUBJECT: "No Second Gear" When Transmission Is At
Operating Temperatures

MODELS AFFECTED: All THM 400 Transmissions.

NOTE: This is a supplement to Bulletin 72-T-31 Group
75-#8 Dated June 13, 1972.

There have been reports of Turbo Hydra-Matic 400 model
transmission that have developed erratic shift patterns
after reaching operating temperature, especially during
warmer weather.

The complaint is described in several ways as such:

Misses second gear.
Transmission hunts 1-3-1.
Shifts 1-3.
Engine flairs on downshift.
Slips in second.
No second except "L2" or "L1".

Experience has shown that these problems can be caused
by an intermediate clutch inner piston seal that loses
its ability to seal when hot. Examination of the intermediate clutch or seal generally shows no distress or
wear.

If a complaint such as those listed above is encountered,
the intermediate clutch piston seals must be replaced.

BUICK DEALER

SERVICE INFORMATION

BULLETIN

Model Year	1973
Bulletin No.	73-I-82
File in Group	40
Number	2
Date	5-10-73

SUBJECT: Revised Axle Usage Chart

MODELS AFFECTED: 1973 "B", "C" and "E" Series

The following axle usage chart is being revised and updated to replace the chart shown on page 4B-49 of the 1973 Buick Chassis Service Manual.

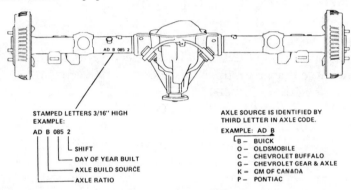

STAMPED LETTERS 3/16" HIGH
EXAMPLE:

AD B 085 2

— SHIFT
— DAY OF YEAR BUILT
— AXLE BUILD SOURCE
— AXLE RATIO

AXLE SOURCE IS IDENTIFIED BY
THIRD LETTER IN AXLE CODE.

EXAMPLE: AD B

B — BUICK
O — OLDSMOBILE
C — CHEVROLET BUFFALO
G — CHEVROLET GEAR & AXLE
K — GM OF CANADA
P — PONTIAC

MODELS	ENGINE	TRANSMISSION	AXLE ASSEMBLY RATIO USAGE								
			STANDARD			ECONOMY (G95)			PERFORMANCE (G92)		
			RATIO	REG CODE	Ltd. CODE SLIP(G80)	RATIO	REG CODE	Ltd.CODE SLIP(G80)	RATIO	REG CODE	Ltd. CODE SLIP (G80)
LeSabre	350	THM 350	3.08	KC	LC	2.73	KA		3.42	KE	LE
Centurion				UC	VC						
	455	THM 400	2.73	UA	VA				3.23	UD	VD
Police Car Option	350	THM 350	3.08	UL	VL				3.42	UN	VN
	455	THM 400	2.73	UJ	VJ				3.23	UM	VW
Estate Wagon	455	THM 400	2.93	NH	RH				3.23	NJ	RJ
Electra	455	THM 400	2.73	NA	RA				3.23	NC	RC
									2.93	NB	RB
Riviera	455	THM 400	2.93	NB	RB				2.23	NC	RC
Riviera (GS)	455	THM 400	2.93	RB	RB				3.23	NC	RC
Riviera STAGE 1		THM 400	3.23		RC						

4B-51

BUICK MOTOR DIVISION • SERVICE DEPARTMENT • FLINT, MICHIGAN 48550

1973 SERIES AND MODEL IDENTIFICATION CHART

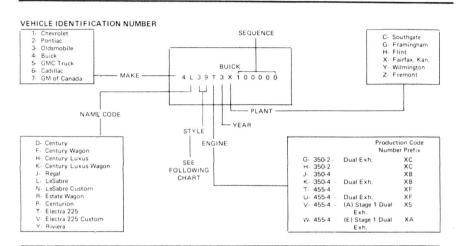

VEHICLE IDENTIFICATION NUMBER

1- Chevrolet	
2- Pontiac	
3- Oldsmobile	
4- Buick	
5- GMC Truck	
6- Cadillac	
7- GM of Canada	

SEQUENCE

BUICK

4 L 39 T 3 X 1 0 0 0 0 0

MAKE

C- Southgate
G- Framingham
H- Flint
X- Fairfax, Kan.
Y- Wilmington
Z- Fremont

NAME CODE — PLANT — YEAR — STYLE — ENGINE

D- Century
F- Century Wagon
H- Century Luxus
K- Century Luxus Wagon
J- Regal
L- LeSabre
N- LeSabre Custom
R- Estate Wagon
P- Centurion
T- Electra 225
V- Electra 225 Custom
Y- Riviera

SEE FOLLOWING CHART

			Production Code Number Prefix
G-	350-2 -	Dual Exh.	XC
H-	350-2		XC
J-	350-4		XB
K-	350-4 -	Dual Exh.	XB
T-	455-4		XF
U-	455-4 -	Dual Exh.	XF
V-	455-4 -	(A) Stage 1 Dual Exh.	XS
W-	455-4 -	(E) Stage 1 Dual Exh.	XA

STANDARD SPECIFICATIONS

SERIES	SALES MODEL NO.	WHEEL-BASE		BODY STYLE	STANDARD			FRONT TREAD	REAR TREAD	OVERALL		
					ENG	TRANS	AXLE			LENGTH	HEIGHT	WIDTH
"A"	4AD37	112.0	37	2-DOOR COUPE	350 2	3-SPD. MAN.	3.08	61.50	60.68	210.1	53.10	77.70
	29	116.0	29	4-DOOR SEDAN 6W						214.1	54.00	
	4AF35	116.0	35	4-DOOR 2-SEAT WAGON						217.9	55.20	
	4AH57	112.0	57	2-DOOR COUPE						210.0	53.10	
	29	116.0	29	4-DOOR SEDAN 6W						214.1	54.00	
	4AK35	116.0	35	4-DOOR 2-SEAT WAGON						217.9	55.20	
	4AJ57	112.0	57	2-DOOR FORMAL COUPE						212.4	53.10	
"B"	4BL57	124.0	57	2-DOOR COUPE HARDTOP	350 2	3-SPD. AUTO.		63.64	64.00	225.3	54.30	80.00
	39		39	4-DOOR HARDTOP								
	69		69	4-DOOR SEDAN T/P								
	4BN57		57	2-DOOR COUPE HARDTOP								
	39		39	4-DOOR HARDTOP								
	69		69	4-DOOR SEDAL T/P								
	4BP57	124.0	57	2-DOOR COUPE HARDTOP	350 4	3-SPD. AUTO.					53.60	
	67		67	2-DOOR CONVERTIBLE								
	39		39	4-DOOR HARDTOP								
	4BR35		35	4-DOOR 2-SEAT WAGON	455 4	3-SPD. AUTO.	2.93			231.0	57.10	
	45		45	4-DOOR 3-SEAT WAGON								
"C"	4CT37	127.0	37	2-DOOR COUPE HARDTOP	455 4	3-SPD. AUTO.	2.73			231.5	54.10	
	39		39	4-DOOR HARDTOP							54.60	
	4CV37		37	2-DOOR COUPE HARDTOP							54.10	
	39		39	4-DOOR HARDTOP							54.60	
"E"	4EY87	122.0	87	2-DOOR COUPE HARDTOP	455 4	3-SPD. AUTO.	2.93			224.4	53.80	

3. 1973 Paint Codes

Color chip sheets for the 1973 Buick paints will again be available from DuPont, Ditzler, and Rinshed-Mason. Each Buick dealer will be sent two copies of each as they are made available to us.

Following is a list of the 1973 Buick exterior colors:

Paint Code	Sales Code	Color Name	DuPont Stock No.	Ditzler Stock No.	Rinshed-Mason Stock No.
11	C	Artic White	5338L	2058	A-2080
19	A	Regal Black	99L	9300	A-946
24	D	Medium Blue Metallic	5473L	5223	A-2623
26	E	Mediterranean Blue	5478L	2524	A-2624
29	F	Midnight Blue	5474L	2526	A-2626
42	G	Jade Green	5489L	2528	A-2628
44	H	Willow Green	5475L	2529	A-2629
46	I	Green-Gold Metallic	5479L	2530	A-2631D
48	J	Midnight Green	5480L	2531	A-2632
54	K	Autumn Gold	5497L	2536	A-2637
56	L	Colonial Yellow	5481L	2537	A-2638
60	M	Harvest Gold	5490L	2538	A-2639D
64	N	Silver Cloud	5476L	2541	A-2643
65	P	Burnt Coral	5554L	2557	A-2644G
66	Q	Taupe Metallic	5482L	2542	A-2645
67	R	Midnight Gray	5553L	2558	A-2646
68	S	Brown Metallic	5483L	2543	A-2647D
74	T	Burgundy	5477L	2545	A-2649F
81	U	Bamboo Cream	5491L	2549	A-2653

Engine	Spark Plug	Plug Gap	Dwell Angle	Breaker Gap	Initial* Timing ± 2°	Curb Idle Speed**		
						IDLE STOP SOLENOID CONNECTED	IDLE STOP SOLENOID DISCONNECTED	FAST IDLE SPEED
350 Engine (Man. Trans.) 4D - 4F - 4G - 4H Series	R45TS	.040"	30° ± 2°	.016"	4° B.T.D.C.	800	600	820
350 Engine (Auto. Trans.) 4D - 4F - 4G - 4H Series W / 2 BBL. Carburetor	R45TS	.040"	30° ± 2°	.016"	4° B.T.D.C.	650	500	700
350 Engine (Auto. Trans.) 4D - 4F - 4G - 4H Series W / 4 BBL. Carb. and 4L - 4N Series W / 2 & 4 BBL.	R45TS	.040"	30° ± 2°	.016"	4° B.T.D.C.	650	500	700
455 Engine (Man. Trans.)	R45TS	.040"	30° ± 2°	.016"	4° B.T.D.C.	900	600	920
455 Engine (Auto. Trans.)	R45TS	.040"	30° ± 2°	.016"	4° B.T.D.C.	650	500	700
455 State 1 (Man. Trans.)	R45TS	.040"	30° ± 2°	.016"	10° B.T.D.C.	900	600	920
455 Stage 1 (Auto. Trans.)	R45TS	.040"	30° ± 2°	.016"	10° B.T.D.C.	650	500	700

*With Hose Disconnected From Vacuum Advance and Plugged.

**With Automatic Transmission in Drive (Manual Transmission in Neutral) — First Set Idle Speed with Idle Stop Solenoid Connected, then with Solenoid Disconnected.

CAUTION: In 1973 all Buick engines will have silicone material spark plug boots which is superior for temperature resistance but lower in tear strength than materials used in the past. Because of the latter the practice of inserting objects under the boot to obtain a terminal for timing light hookup cannot be tolerated.

The recommended practice is to use either an adapter between the spark plug and the wire or an induction pick-up device that clamps to the wire.

Model Year	1973
Bulletin No.	73-I-103
File in Group	58
Number	6
Date	6-15-73

SUBJECT: Initial Timing of Stage I Engines

MODELS AFFECTED: 1973 "A", "B" and "E" Series

Some confusion exists as to correct intial timing
specification of 1973 Stage I engines. The correct
timing specification is as follows:

$$\text{"A" Series} \quad 10° \pm 2°$$
$$\text{"B" and "E" Series} \quad 4° \pm 2°$$

This information supersedes all specification previously printed in the 1973 Buick Chassis Service
Manual.

BUICK MOTOR DIVISION • **SERVICE DEPARTMENT** • **FLINT, MICHIGAN 48550**

BUICK ENGINE TUNE-UP AND EMISSIONS CONTROL SPECIFICATIONS 1965-1973

YEAR	ENGINE	CARB.	TRANS.	EMISSIONS CONTROL DEVICES	SPARK PLUG	PLUG GAP (INCH)	TIMING (DEGREES)	IDLE SPEED
'65	225	—	—	PCV	44S	.035	5	550 (1)
	300 Special	2bbl.	—	PCV	45S	.035	5	550 (1)
	300 Special	4bbl.	—	PCV	44S	.035	5	550 (1)
	300 LeSabre	2bbl.	—	PCV	45S	.035	2½	550 (1)
	300 LeSabre	4bbl.	—	PCV	44S	.035	2½	550 (1)
	400	4bbl.	—	PCV	44S	.035	2½	500 (1)
	401	4bbl.	—	PCV	44S	.035	2½	500 (1)
	425	4bbl.	—	PCV	44S	.035	2½	500 (1)
	425	2-4bbl.	Manual	PCV	44S	.035	2½	500 (1)
	425	2-4bbl.	Auto	PCV	44S	.035	12	500 (1)
'66	225	—	—	PCV-*A.I.R.	44S	.035	5	550 (1)
	300	2bbl.	—	PCV-*A.I.R.	45S	.035	2½	550 (1)
	300	4bbl.	—	PCV-*A.I.R.	44S	.035	2½	550 (1)
	340	2bbl.	—	PCV-*A.I.R.	45S	.035	2½	550 (1)
	340	4bbl.	—	PCV-*A.I.R.	44S	.035	2½	550 (1)
	400	—	—	PCV-*A.I.R.	44S	.035	2½	500 (1)
	401	—	—	PCV-*A.I.R.	44S	.035	2½	500 (1)
	425	—	—	PCV-*A.I.R.	44S	.035	2½	500 (1)
	425	2-4bbl.	—	PCV-*A.I.R.	44S	.035	12	500 (1)
'67	225	—	—	PCV-*A.I.R.	44S	.035	5	550 (1)
	300	2bbl.	—	PCV-*A.I.R.	45S	.035	2½	550 (1)
	340	2bbl.	—	PCV-*A.I.R.	45S	.035	2½	550 (1)
	340	4bbl.	—	PCV-*A.I.R.	44S	.035	2½	550 (1)
	400	—	—	PCV-*A.I.R.	44TS	.035	2½	550 (1)
	430	—	—	PCV-*A.I.R.	44TS	.035	2½	550 (1)
'68	250	—	Manual	PCV-CCS	46N	.030	0	700
	250	—	Auto	PCV-CCS	46N	.030	4	500
	350	—	Auto	PCV-CCS	45TS	.030	0	550
	400	—	Auto	PCV-CCS	44TS	.030	0	550
	430	—	Auto	PCV-CCS	44TS	.030	0	550
	All V-8	—	Manual	PCV-CCS	—	.030	0	700
'69	250	—	Manual	PCV-CCS	R46N	.035	0	700
	250	—	Auto	PCV-CCS	R46N	.035	4	500 (2)
	350	—	Manual	PCV-CCS	R45TS	.030	0	700
	350	—	Auto	PCV-CCS	R45TS	.030	0	600
	400	—	Manual	PCV-CCS	R44TS	.030	2½ A.T.D.C.	700
	400	—	Auto	PCV-CCS	R44TS	.030	0	600
	430	—	Auto	PCV-CCS	R44TS	.030	0	550
'70	250	—	Manual	PCV-CCS-*EEC-TCS	R46T	.035	0	750
	250	—	Auto	PCV-CCS-*EEC-TCS	R46T	.035	4	600 (2)
	350	—	Manual	PCV-CCS-*EEC	R45TS	.030	6	700
	350	—	Auto	PCV-CCS-*EEC	R45TS	.030	6	600
	455	—	Manual	PCV-CCS-*EEC-TCS	R44TS	.030	6	700
	455	—	Auto	PCV-CCS-*EEC-TCS	R44TS	.030	6	600
	455	Stage 1	Manual	PCV-CCS-*EEC-TCS	R44TS	.030	10	700
	455	Stage 1	Auto	PCV-CCS-*EEC-TCS	R44TS	.030	10	600
'71	250	—	Manual	PCV-CCS-TCS-EEC	R46TS	.035	4	550
	250	—	Auto	PCV-CCS-TCS-EEC	R46TS	.035	4	500
	350	—	Manual	PCV-CCS-TCS-EEC	R45TS	.030	6	800
	350	(4)	Auto	PCV-CCS-TCS-EEC	R45TS	.030	10	600
	350	(5)	Auto	PCV-CCS-TCS-EEC	R45TS	.030	4	600
	455	—	Manual	PCV-CCS-TCS-EEC	R44TS	.030	6	700
	455	—	Auto	PCV-CCS-TCS-EEC	R44TS	.030	4	600
	455	Stage 1	Manual	PCV-CCS-TCS-EEC	R44TS	.030	10	700
	455	Stage 1	Auto	PCV-CCS-TCS-EEC	R44TS	.030	10	600
'72	350	—	Manual	PCV-CCS-TCS-EEC-A.I.R.-**EGR	R45TS	.040	4	800-600 (3)
	350	—	Auto	PCV-CCS-TCS-EEC-*A.I.R.-**EGR	R45TS	.040	4	650-500 (3)
	455	—	Manual	PCV-CCS-TCS-EEC-A.I.R.-**EGR	R45TS	.040	4	900-600 (3)
	455	—	Auto	PCV-CCS-TCS-EEC-A.I.R.-**EGR	R45TS	.040	4	650-500 (3)
	455	Stage 1	Manual	PCV-CCS-TCS-EEC-A.I.R.-**EGR	R45TS	.040	8	900-600 (3)
	455	Stage 1	Auto	PCV-CCS-TCS-EEC-A.I.R.-**EGR	R45TS	.040	10	650-500 (3)
'73	250	—	Manual	PCV-CCS-TCS-EEC-A.I.R.-EGR	R46T	.035	6	700-500 (3)
	250	—	Auto	PCV-CCS-EEC-A.I.R.-EGR	R46T	.035	6	600-500 (3)
	350	—	Manual	PCV-CCS-TCS-EEC-A.I.R.-EGR	R45TS	.040	4	800-600 (3)
	350	—	Auto	PCV-CCS-EEC-A.I.R.-EGR	R45TS	.040	4	650-500 (3)
	455	—	Manual	PCV-CCS-TCS-ECC-A.I.R.-EGR	R45TS	.040	4	900-600 (3)
	455	—	Auto	PCV-CCS-EEC-A.I.R.-EGR	R45TS	.040	4	650-500 (3)
	455	Stage 1	Manual	PCV-CCS-TCS-EEC-A.I.R.-EGR	R45TS	.040	10	900-600 (3)
	455	Stage 1	Auto	PCV-CCS-TCS-EEC-A.I.R.-EGR	R45TS	.040	10	650-500 (3)

BUICK DEALER

SERVICE INFORMATION

BULLETIN

Model Year	1973
Bulletin No.	73-I-23
File in Group	60
Number	1
Date	11-21-72

SUBJECT: 455 Cubic Inch Basic Engine Cylinder Head Gasket Usage

MODELS AFFECTED: 1970, 1971 and 1972

This bulletin is being issued to give more coverage to Parts and Accessory Bulletin 72-9. Listed below are the basic engines by Part Number, year and the gasket usage.

Basic Engine - Group 0.033
1394850 - 1970-1971 455 Engine, Except Stage I
1394851 - 1971-1972 455 Engine Stage I
1394989 - 1972   455 Engine, Except Stage I

Current shipments of the above Basic Engines may include "oblong" casting cleanout holes to the cylinder head as compared to "round" holes in the original equipment engine block.

Refer to the following illustration for quick means of visual identification.

CAUTION: If the Basic Engines have the "double scallop" per illustration and the "oblong" holes, do not use the 1970-1972 Cylinder Head Gasket, 1237849. Use new Cylinder Head Gasket, 1241749.

If the above Basic Engines have the "single scallop" per illustration and the "round" holes, the specified Cylinder Head Gasket, 1237849, for 1970-1972 models may be used, or the 1973 Gasket, 1241749, may be used optionally as available.

IMPORTANT: Inspect each of the above Basic Engines in stock or as received and supply the correct Cylinder Head Gasket. Water loss into the oil can result if an incorrect Gasket is used.

BUICK MOTOR DIVISION • SERVICE DEPARTMENT • FLINT, MICHIGAN 48550

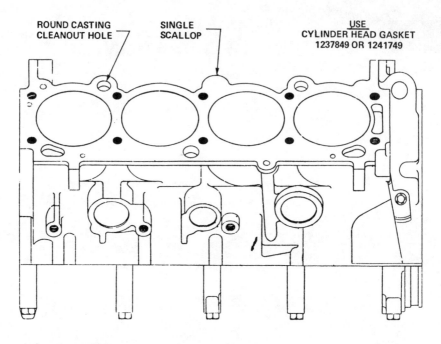

ROUND CASTING
CLEANOUT HOLE

SINGLE
SCALLOP

USE
CYLINDER HEAD GASKET
1237849 OR 1241749

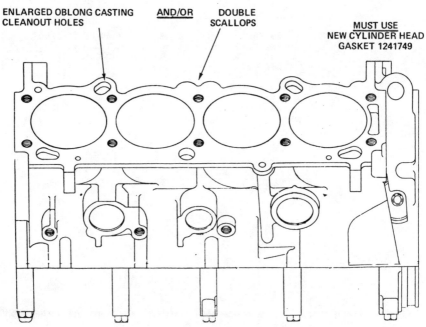

ENLARGED OBLONG CASTING
CLEANOUT HOLES

AND/OR

DOUBLE
SCALLOPS

MUST USE
NEW CYLINDER HEAD
GASKET 1241749

BUICK DEALER

SERVICE INFORMATION

BULLETIN

Model Year	1973
Bulletin No.	73-I-106
File in Group	64
Number	4
Date	6-15-73

SUBJECT: Accelerator Pump Adjustment, 4MV Quadrajet
Carburetor

MODELS AFFECTED: 1973 455 and 350 Cubic Inch Engines

The accelerator pump on the Rochester 4MV Carburetor very seldom requires any service adjustment. When accelerator pump plunger stem height is found to be out of specifications, it indicates that the pump rod is in the wrong hole in the pump lever, rather than the pump lever being misadjusted.

NOTE: If an accelerator pump adjustment is found to be necessary, care must be taken so as not to twist the pump lever or bend the pump rod, as it may cause binding of the accelerator linkage when the twisted or bent parts begin to wear.

The following specifications replace those shown on page 6E-144 of the 1973 Buick Chassis Service Manual:

	455 Automatic Transmission A-B-C-E Series	455 Manual Transmission A Series	455 Stage 1 Automatic and Manual Transmission A Series
Pump Rod Location	Inner	Inner	Inner
Pump Adjustment	1/4"	1/4"	1/4"

	350 Automatic Transmission A-B-X Series	350 Manual Transmission A Series
Pump Rod Location	Outer	Inner
Pump Adjustment	3/8"	9/32"

BUICK MOTOR DIVISION • **SERVICE DEPARTMENT** • **FLINT, MICHIGAN 48550**

BUICK DEALER

SERVICE INFORMATION

BULLETIN

Model Year	1973
Bulletin No.	73-I-51
File in Group	00
Number	12
Date	2-14-73

SUBJECT: Glove Box Label - Fuel Recommendations

MODELS AFFECTED: 1973

Starting in January, 1973, all General Motors passenger cars and light duty trucks will have the label (illustrated below) affixed to the inner glove box door panel which recommends the use of unleaded or low-lead gasoline of at least 91 Research Octane.

HOW TO SELECT THE PROPER GASOLINE FOR PERFORMANCE • ECONOMY • ECOLOGY

This vehicle is designed to operate on unleaded or low-lead fuels of at least 91 Research Octane. These fuels will minimize spark plug fouling and emission system deterioration. Leaded regular fuels containing more than 0.5 grams of lead per gallon normally should not be used. The engine does not require premium fuel. Therefore, its use would be an unnecessary additional expense.

If the service station gas pump has a symbol similar to the sample below, preferably use unleaded or low-lead gasoline with a symbol number of 2. A higher number is satisfactory but not required.

Ask your gasoline dealer for information on the fuel you are using both as to lead content and octane rating.

PRINTED IN U.S.A.   PT. NO. 339203

Dealership personnel should acquaint owners with this label and encourage them to follow the recommendations included since use of unleaded or low-lead fuels will provide the following important benefits

1. Reduce vehicle emissions - An immediate small reduction in the emission of exhaust hydrocarbons results, as well as a reduction in combustion chamber lead deposits which cause hydrocarbon emissions to increase with mileage. Also, the emission of lead-containing particles is reduced.

2. Increase spark plug life - Lead deposits which form on spark plugs are electrical conductors which eventually short out plugs. This shows up as a loss in fuel economy, performance and emission control. Use of unleaded fuels can greatly extend spark plug life.

3. Increase exhaust system life - Lead salts are corrosive. The use of unleaded fuel will greatly extend exhaust system life.

4. Reduce engine rusting - Engine oil contamination is reduced by using unleaded fuels, extending the protection against engine rusting.

BUICK MOTOR DIVISION   •   SERVICE DEPARTMENT   •   FLINT, MICHIGAN 48550

BUICK DEALER

SERVICE INFORMATION

BULLETIN

Model Year	1973
Bulletin No.	73-I-29
File in Group	100
Number	3
Date	12-19-72

SUBJECT: Exchanging of Radial Ply Tires From One Car to Another

MODELS AFFECTED: 1973

For 1973, Buick is offering steel belted radial ply tires on the Electra, Riviera, Gran Sport and Regal. The new Riviera G.S. comes with these tires as standard equipment.

To ensure maximum customer satisfaction, Buicks equipped with steel belted radial ply tires are specifically tuned for the unique ride and handling characteristics of these tires.

It is strongly urged that exchanges not be made between cars with radial tires and those with conventional tires.

The benefits of steel belted radial ply tire construction are well known and include higher tread mileage, improved fuel economy, and improved traction and handling capability. But the full range of benefits is only achieved when the car is modified to make best use of the tires, including:

- Special Body Mounting System

- Revised Structural Characteristics

- Tailored Shock Absorbers

- Special Rear Suspension Arms

For more sporty handling, the Gran Sport and Riviera G.S. have further suspension modifications:

- High rate front and rear springs

- Larger, one (1") inch diameter front stabilizer bar

- Rear Stabilizer Bar

A car not tuned to radial tires will suffer a ride penalty if radial tires are installed. Likewise, if conventional tires are installed on a car that has been factory equipped with radial ply tires, a harsh ride with possible shake may result. In either case, the result may be a dissatisfied customer.

BUICK MOTOR DIVISION • SERVICE DEPARTMENT • FLINT, MICHIGAN 48550

BUICK DEALER

SERVICE INFORMATION

BULLETIN

Model Year	1973
Bulletin No.	73-I-44
File in Group	68
Number	3
Date	1-31-73

SUBJECT: Erratic Operation of Cruise Control

MODELS AFFECTED: 1973

If a vehicle is equipped with cruise control and automatic level control (A.L.C.), it is very important
that the proper hose routing be maintained. The A.L.C.
vacuum supply hose to the compressor must be connected
to the PCV valve hose by a "T". Erratic operation of
the cruise control may be encountered if the vacuum
source for the A.L.C. system is not at the PCV valve.
See illustration for proper hose routing.

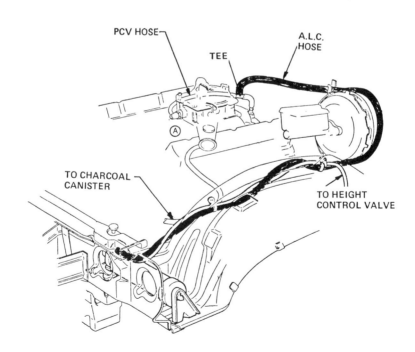

BUICK MOTOR DIVISION • SERVICE DEPARTMENT • FLINT, MICHIGAN 48550

RIVIERA
SOURCE SECTION

The following section is included to help guide you to Businesses and Clubs that may be able to help you in some way with your Riviera. All the companies in this section are reputable and many are very well known.

We think that putting a section in this book for a few advertisers is a good way for them to let you, the Riviera owner know what services they have to offer, in their own words.

PURELY GRAND NATIONAL!

Buick Gran Sport Club of America

The **GSCA** was formed in 1982 and has been aggressively promoting Buick Musclecars ever since! When we first started our club, Buick's only Musclecar was the Gran Sport. But in 1984, Buick struck again with the fantastic Grand Nationals; and as they say, the rest is history! Today, most of our members own one or the other, a GS or a GN! Many members own both as well as other Buicks!! And then there's the *GS X-tra* . . . .

PURELY GRAN SPORT, DEFINITELY!

In the **GS X-TRA,** our bi-monthly newsletter, we continuously evaluate Buick performance items and are able to offer suggestions on the ultimate performance pieces for the GS and GN. We are always free to tell it like it is. We do a lot of product testing in order to save you time and money on knowing what and what not to buy! The GS X-tra is packed full of the best of the best information; and then there's the .....

PURELY BEAUTIFUL!

. . . GS/GN Nationals. Every year in May, we go to Bowling Green, KY and have the best Buick meet around. For 4 full days with over 1000 Buick Musclecars and over 20 different classes, we test, tune, race and have more fun than you could believe. It is one awesome event that rivals any other car meet in the world. But all of this is only part of what the GS Club has to offer. Give us a call, this is where the action is when it comes to (all) Buick musclecars!!!

PURELY BAD!

Purely Awesome! Purely Great! Purely Outrageous! Purely Exciting! Purely Radical! Purely Fasssssst!! *Purely the # 1 Buick Club around!!!* Call us at **(912) 244-0577** or join now by sending $30.00 for a 1 year membership! **Send to:** *GSCA*   **1213 Gornto Rd. Dept. EB**   **Valdosta, GA 31602**

Hear what Buick GSCA members say about the club . . .

YEAR ONE
4"54-D N. Royal Atlanta Dr.
Tucker, GA 30084
(404) 493-6568

Dear Richard:

I would like to solicit your help in locating some items that we would like to reproduce for the GS owners. Specifically, we would like to find the GS and GSX grill nameplates for the '70—2 models. I believe that there is some interchangability between some years but am not quite sure which — any help would be appreciated!

Keep up the good work with the club, yours is still the only newsletter I actually read from cover-to-cover anymore.

Sincerely,
Len J. Athanasiades,
President

Dear Richard and the Staff

I was really getting tired of being put down by all the Chevy freaks just because I really like Buicks, but by joining the GSCA I found out that there are those like myself who simply know a great car when they see it. I've found that our club is more like a family and everyone is eager to help each other. Thank you for putting it all together; it's one super organization.

Dal Burton
Atlanta, GA

January 1, 1988

Dear GSCA.

I had to let you know the results of my 455 build-up that we discussed over the phone. Thanks to your excellent advice on parts selection my "baby" is running great. Remember the guy with the big buck 454 Chevelle I told you about? Well, he's history after a back-road race the other night. He sure knows what a Buick is now! All his friends were there too. Boy Thanks so much for all your help. Boy did it work. Count me in as a member for life!

Gary Schwarz
San Mateo, CA

Hello!

I'd also like to say that as a new member I have found the club newsletter to be invaluable. This is in contrast to the ███████ Newsletter which, save for a couple of issues, has been disappointing. I don't think I will be renewing my subscription when I can get twice as much information & entertainment from one GSCA Newsletter than from four issues of "███████."

Well anyway, keep up the good work. I am proudly displaying my club sticker and I couldn't do it without your help.

Sincerely
Chris Beeks #820
Bellevue, WA

December 1, 1987

Hello GSCA

You guys are doing a great job in helping us Turbo Regal owners. I subscribe to two other publications involving turbo tips for these cars but will not re-subscribe when I can get much more honest info from your publication. All these other guys just want to sell you their products. You've saved me a bundle already thru your absolutely excellent tech advice. I attended last year's "Nationals" and it was simply unreal. You guys do a fantastic job.

Kelly Williams
Salt Lake City, UT

Dear Richard,

We really had a good time doing the GS Stage 2 article on Jim Turner's 10-second street GS. Thanks for help in proofing it. And by the way, I think that your GS X-tra is one of the very best club magazines (and we get 'em all). The technical coverage is really great which is something a member of any club should expect but rarely receives.

Lee Beck; Staff Writer
Musclecars of the '60's / 70's
Sidney, OH 45365

Mr. Lasseter

Our GS X-tra just saved me a lot of troubles and money! I had a problem with my 1987 GN that I diagnosed easily through the excellent information contained in our publication. I had written to another club who supposedly knew about these things but they were unable to help. It's great to be among the sharpest turbo GN and T-type owners in the country. I'm also avidly looking now for an older GS Buick to restore. Thanks to this very professional club and its members, I'm really enjoying my Buicks to the fullest.

Continued Success
Charles Merrill, Jr.
Midland, TX

Rich —

I just wanted to tell you how impressed I am with the GSCA newsletter. Having been in the auto hobby and business for over 25 years and belonging to many clubs, your magazine is the best, and so far as a new member I've only received two issues.

I am new to the Buick part of the GM clan but have owned a '65 GTO for over 23 years and I've co-authored the GTO Restoration Guide with Paul Zazarine.

Since purchasing an '87 GN I feel like a novice, so I'm ordering the back issue packet while waiting for my next magazine. I'm also looking forward to attending the GS Nationals in Bowling Green.

Keep up the good work!

Chuck Roberts
Laurel, MD

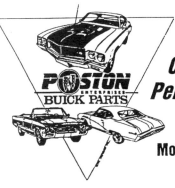